TOTALLY CHAOTIC HISTORY
ROMAN BRITAIN GETS ROWDY!

First published 2024 by Walker Books Ltd
87 Vauxhall Walk, London SE11 5HJ

2 4 6 8 10 9 7 5 3 1

Text © 2024 Greg Jenner
Illustrations © 2024 Rikin Parekh

The right of Greg Jenner and Rikin Parekh to be identified as author and illustrator respectively of this work has been asserted in accordance with the Copyright, Designs and Patents Act 1988

This book has been typeset in Adobe Garamond Pro

Printed by CPI Group (UK) Ltd, Croydon, CR0 4YY

All rights reserved. No part of this book may be reproduced, transmitted or stored in an information retrieval system in any form or by any means, graphic, electronic or mechanical, including photocopying, taping and recording, without prior written permission from the publisher.

British Library Cataloguing in Publication Data: a catalogue record for this book is available from the British Library

ISBN 978-1-4063-9566-2

www.walker.co.uk

GREG JENNER

with **Dr EMMA SOUTHON**

illustrated by RIKIN PAREKH

WALKER BOOKS

WELCOME TO ROMAN BRITAIN!

Hello! I assume you're here because you want to know more about Roman Britain, right? Well, you've chosen wisely. This book is so chock-a-block full of ancient stuff, you'll soon have knowledge leaking out of your ears, like jam oozing from a doughnut! You'll find out about marching legionaries, luxury villas and Hadrian's Wall. But watch out! This book isn't going to be a boring list of facts, because it's really about …

(… and also Roman Britain)

Hi! I'm Greg, and I'm a public historian – that means my job is to make history fun. And in this book I'm going to propel you through the unpredictable story of how Britain was conquered and changed by the Romans (until they abandoned it!).

Be warned: this will be a wild ride. At one point, nineteen Roman emperors in a row will meet a sticky end! Watch out for my chaos meter – it will tell you how cheerfully calm or calamitously chaotic things are:

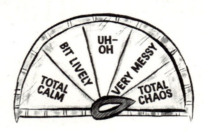

And we won't be on this journey alone! Let me introduce you to my mega-brainy co-author, Dr Emma Southon, who is an expert ancient historian. While I pull you through the story at super-speed, Emma will be here to tell us which events *are* true, which *might* be true, and which are just a bunch of fanciful myths. We might even have a big ol' argument about rival theories, but don't worry – passionate debate is CLASSIC

That's me!

HISTORIAN BEHAVIOUR, and we'll still be pals afterwards! Listen out for Emma's accuracy alarm as we go along.

BEEEEEEEP!

I'm also totally going to scribble all over the margins – I have loads of facts to share with you!

WHAT HAPPENS NEXT?!

You might think that history is just loads of yawn-worthy dates and confusing names that seem to be spelled by an angry cat stomping on a computer keyboard. Sure, some names are tricky – like Tiberius Claudius ~~Cogydumbnus~~ ~~Cogidlunchbus~~ Cogidubnus – but it's not all about that. What if we stopped thinking of Roman Britain as being ages ago and imagined what it would actually be like to live through it? We wouldn't think of ourselves as ancient; we'd be MODERN! And we'd have no idea what was coming next – no clue if there'd be a rebellion on Wednesday, a new emperor on Thursday, or an army of giant radioactive hamsters attacking major cities at the weekend! Historians study stuff after it's happened – they know what comes next – but when you're living through the chaos, *tomorrow* is ??????

Third time lucky, Greg!

Er ... WHAT?!

That's what you're going to experience in this book. Prepare to be rocketed through a thousand years of TOTAL CHAOS. Hold on tight!

SO YOU THINK YOU KNOW ROMAN BRITAIN?

Here's a question for you – what do you think of when I say Roman Britain? Perhaps these are some of the things that pop into your mind…

JULIUS CAESAR

SUMPTUOUS VILLAS

BOUDICA

STRAIGHT ROADS

And none of those are wrong! But the history of Roman Britain is messier than you probably realize. For example, did you know that…

- Hadrian wasn't the only emperor to build a famous wall – so did a ruler called Antoninus Pius.
- Some Roman writers thought Julius Caesar's invasion of Britain was a total waste of time!
- Boudica wasn't the only warrior queen in ancient Britain (and we don't know if that was her actual name!).

There's so much chaos for us to race through, but don't panic – it's going to be epic! We'll start 2,800 years ago, in the Iron Age, and then hurtle through 1,200 years of invasions, rebellions, murdered emperors and loads of fish gut sauce (I'll explain later!). Once we're done, you'll never see Roman Britain in the same way again. To help you get to grips with it all, here's a handy timeline…

TIMELINE OF

100 BCE
Roman stuff arrives in Iron Age Britain thanks to traders from Gaul.

55–54 BCE
Roman leader Julius Caesar invades Britain twice, but soon goes home.

43 CE
Emperor Claudius conquers southern Britain.

286 CE
Roman commander Carausius declares himself independent emperor of Britain! He is later murdered by his adviser, Allectus.

235 CE
Crisis of the Third Century. The Roman Empire is in political and financial chaos!

293 CE
Emperor Diocletian splits the Roman Empire in half, with each half co-ruled by a senior and junior emperor.

296 CE
Allectus is killed. Britain is returned to Roman control and split into four provinces.

306 CE
Constantine the Great is crowned emperor in Eboracum (York).

313 CE
Constantine makes Christianity legal in the Roman Empire.

367 CE
The Great Conspiracy: Britain is attacked from all sides by foreign enemies possibly working together.

ROMAN BRITAIN

50 CE
British king Caratacus leads the resistance in the west of Britain (modern Wales), but is captured by the Romans.

60-61 CE
Queen Boudica rebels, and destroys several Roman towns! She is defeated at the Battle of Watling Street.

78 CE
The Romans conquer the western area of Britain (modern Wales).

85 CE
Vindolanda Fort is built on the northern border of Roman Britain.

122 CE
Construction of Hadrian's Wall begins.

142 CE
Antoninus Pius builds another wall further north. It doesn't last long.

193 CE
Year of the Five Emperors. Murder and civil war rock the Roman Empire!

211 CE
Emperor Septimius Severus splits Britain into two provinces, but dies after fighting the Caledonians in the north.

383 CE
Wannabe emperor Magnus Maximus borrows Britain's soldiers for his civil war, leaving the country largely undefended.

c.400 CE
Britain has money troubles: trade collapses, coin hoards are buried and towns fall into disrepair.

407 CE
Constantine III declares himself emperor and leaves Britain, taking most remaining Roman soldiers with him.

409 CE
Rome abandons Britain for ever.

So, that's what Roman Britain's history looks like to historians ... but how did it feel to <u>live</u> through it? Let's jump back in time to find out for ourselves – and to set the scene properly, we'll begin in the Iron Age, to discover who the Britons were BEFORE the Romans even showed up. But, be warned: with 800 years to cram in, we'll need to go fast, so hang on tight!

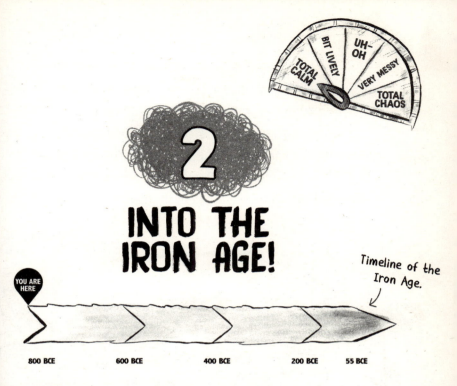

2
INTO THE IRON AGE!

Timeline of the Iron Age.

YOU ARE HERE

800 BCE   600 BCE   400 BCE   200 BCE   55 BCE

Welcome to ancient Britain, 2,800 years ago – and there's not a Roman to be seen anywhere! Let's get familiar with our surroundings, shall we? Great Britain is one of the <u>two big islands</u> in the so-called British Isles. People have lived here for thousands of years, but here in the Iron Age, they are finally learning how to <u>get the wrinkles out of their clothes</u>…

I live on the other big island, Ireland.

JUST JOKING!!! Nah, it's when people learn to make strong tools and weapons by <u>smelting</u> iron (which is stronger than bronze). What's Iron Age Britain like, then? Well, everyone is living in

Stop being silly, Greg – it's not the Ironing Age!

Heating iron ore in a furnace.

13

They're about 8 metres wide in the Early Iron Age, with a fireplace, no windows, and 10-20 people living together – cosy but smoky!

scattered homesteads (farms), and building roundhouses made of wood or stone, with thatched roofs. The types of house vary by region, but they all have that round shape, which suggests these Britons share a culture— Uh … hang on a sec! Who are these *Britons*? Don't we usually call them *Celts*, Emma?

CELTIC CONFUSION

This is a biggie, Greg! 'Celtic' can mean different things: a group of ancient languages; a group of people described by the Greeks and Romans; a name for the early Irish Christian Church; a modern idea of a shared culture between Ireland, Wales, Scotland and Brittany (in northern France); a famous football team from Scotland.

Ancient writers couldn't agree where the Celts were from. One said France, one said Spain and Germany, another said NOT Britain – but Roman leader Julius Caesar said it WAS Britain! Who was right? Modern experts have three theories: Celts came from Germany and moved westwards OR Celts came from the west and moved eastwards OR Celts came from France and moved in every direction! Annoyingly, all three might be true?! HOWEVER we have ZERO evidence that people in ancient Britain ever called themselves Celts. So I don't think we should either. Let's call them *Britons*. Deal?

Deal! WOW, that was SO confusing! That's why we need experts to sort this stuff out for us! My head hurts. Can we please get back to living in the Iron Age?

MOVING ON UP

OK, so we've got our Britons – NOT CELTS! – and they're suddenly having to deal with colder and wetter weather. Do they invent umbrellas? Nope! They instead start building hill forts, which means digging big ditches to surround hills with chunky banks of soil. It takes loads of effort, so why do it? Are these defences to keep people out? Yes, maybe?! Or are they building big stuff to show off? Uh … also, yes?!

This is great, but I'm still wet!

Archaeologists have been debating this for decades! The "showing-off" theory is most popular right now.

The Britons don't drag all their furniture uphill and move into these fancy new forts. Hill forts aren't homes; they're special places to hang out in the summer, have feasts, do religious rituals and exchange ideas. Most people are living elsewhere for the rest of the year, and—

SORRY, SORRY, I've just got to double-check. We're definitely saying they're *not* Celts? Are they not speaking a Celtic language to each other?

ACCURACY ALARM

SAY WHAT?

Oh, this is VERY complicated, Greg! There are so-called 'Celtic' languages spoken today that are actually much older than the Celts, so it's not a helpful name! We group these modern languages into two categories: Brythonic (Welsh, Breton and Cornish) or Goidelic (Irish Gaelic, Manx and Scottish Gaelic). Experts think people in Iron Age Britain probably spoke ancient Brythonic in the south, east and west, and ancient Goidelic in the north.

Riiiiiigggght ... yeah, I wish I hadn't asked! Let's get back to the story.

Now we're into the Middle Iron Age – HUZZAH! The weather improves and people celebrate by getting much better at farming – HUZZAH AGAIN! This means they're producing more food, which means people can support bigger families, which means the population grows, which means they need to build more homes, which means – can I get a trumpet parp, please? –

TOOOOT TOOOOT!

even bigger hill forts!

Some hill forts now triple in size, with greater defences and more space for people and animals inside. Archaeologists call these beefed-up examples Developed Hill Forts which is … well, it's a rubbish name, isn't it? Honestly, can't we call them Hill Forts Max! Or Ultra Forts? What about Chill Forts? No? Urgh, fine…

Hill forts started to increase in size around 400 BCE.

WHAT'S LIFE LIKE FOR BRITONS?

Of course, what we really want to know about Iron Age Britain is: what were the snacks like? Well, they chomp lots of mutton and beef, and pork on special occasions, and even venison (deer). But they don't eat chicken or hare, and – weirdly – only people in the very north-west of the island seem to eat fish and seafood, even though Britain is an island surrounded by sea! Other tasty foods include veggies, eggs, milk and cheese, all of which sounds like what I eat in the 21st century. Oh, and they grow loads of cereal crops to make bread and porridge, and they store spare grain in underground pits so it keeps for a long time without rotting. Smart!

Eating fish? That will NEVER catch on!

Inside the hill forts, people seem happy to work together, with everyone sharing the important jobs: making metal tools, glass and pottery; farming crops; looking after the animals; repairing buildings; and generally keeping busy! Sounds nice, actually.

We used to think this was a time of war, as we found skeletons with weapon injuries, but new evidence suggests very few hill forts were attacked.

That is, until it all starts to fall apart. Suddenly we get into the Late Iron Age, and these previously peaceful people start making their swords longer and going to war with other groups, slinging rocks and clay bullets at each other using swirly whirly hand-held slings! Oh dear, it was all going so well...

YES, BUT WHERE ARE THE ROMANS?!

All right, all right, no need to shout! While all this is happening in Britain, the Romans have been transforming themselves from a small, scrappy town of nobodies into a major power. They've not only conquered Italy, they've started kicking some serious butt in North Africa, Greece and France. They're not near Britain yet, so calm down. But I'm pretty sure it won't be long until we hear from them!

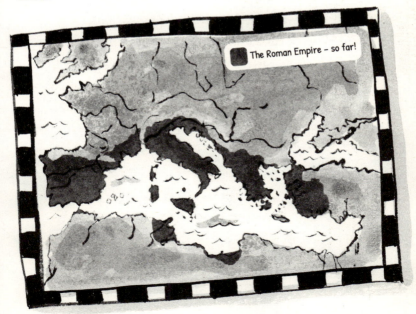

The Roman Empire – so far!

BROCHS AND BURIALS

Where was I? Oh yeah, the Britons! It's tempting to say they're all the same, but they're not. Let's head up to the north of Britain's mainland (and its gaggle of nearby islands), where things look quite different.

Here we find buildings completely unlike anything else in the rest of Britain. The locals are upgrading their homes into huge stone brochs to fit more people in! Brochs are only found in the very north of the island. Imagine those long pepper-shakers that waiters bring you in Italian restaurants ... but now make it thirteen metres tall, and built from a drystone wall! It's by far the cleverest engineering achievement on the whole island. What a way to literally live it *up*!

They were the tallest buildings in Britain at this time

In what we now call Scotland.

We're gonna live like broch stars!

Another obvious difference between groups in the north and south is how they treat their dead. Some Iron Age communities bury their dead (only to dig them up later!), while others leave the bodies out in the open for crows to eat. But if you go <u>two-thirds up</u> ← *What is now Yorkshire.* the island, they have started burying their loved ones with nice objects in the grave. Some women get buried with mirrors, and some men get swords and shields. In fact, the fanciest men and women <u>get buried inside a chariot!</u> Clearly, not everyone is equal in this particular community, otherwise they'd ALL get lovely chariot burials, right?! Perhaps we're seeing the emergence of leaders?

Perhaps the most exciting discovery was at Burnby Lane, in Pocklington, where a young man was buried inside a chariot, next to two horses.

There's a real divide appearing between the north and south of Britain: in what people build, their (customs,) and their language. And this is about to get even more obvious. Remember those Romans rampaging across Europe? They're now in Gaul, the area of western Europe just across the Channel from Britain, and – at last – Roman influence is starting to creep into southern Britain…

Traditional ways of doing everyday things, as well as religious behaviour.

3

THE NORTH/ SOUTH DIVIDE

800 BCE   600 BCE   400 BCE   200 BCE   55 BCE

We've reached 100 BCE, and although the terrifying Roman army remains far away, Roman influence in Britain is growing. The Romans have been busily trading and invading their way through Gaul, which means exotic Roman stuff is ending up in the hands of Gaulish merchants. And guess who likes to pop across the sea and do loads of shopping in northern Gaul? Southern Britons!

Modern-day France, Belgium and Luxembourg.

This has led to lots of changes in the south. I wonder what people from the north make of it all? If only they had mobile phones so we could find out!

22

Hey, Gran, I'm visiting down south. Whoa, u won't believe it! 😳 Boring homesteads GONE! They've levelled up big time, with bangin busy villages and massive hill forts. You gotta see the huge strong gates. Life here is 🔥!

Urgh, sounds horridly cramped! I hope you're doing your traditional religious rituals at home?

Naaah, Gran! They got these sweet new shrines in town and near rivers. Great to get out the house – I love the outdoor vibes 😃!

Disgraceful. And I bet their food is awful!

😂 No, it's taaasty! Pork ain't just for special occasions no more. They got a sauce called garum made from rotten fish guts, u gotta try it. And bitter little fruits called olives, and spices that make your tongue go 😋, and sour alcoholic grape juice called wine … it's proper bussin!

Revolting! I'll stick to mutton and beer, thank you very much!

 Yo, Gran, check out my new haul!!! Pottery made on a revolving wheel, metal and glass drinking cups, personal grooming kit. They got loads here. U want some make-up for your face, Gran?

 What's wrong with my face?!

 😄 Er … nuffin! But u know who has got a nice face? The KING! He's put it on coins, for real!

 COIN?! KING?! Stop making up nonsense words! Have you banged your head, child?

 Don't get it twisted, Gran! Kings are the new leaders down here. And coins are like lil metal discs that u use to buy stuff. It's the latest tech.

 What's wrong with swapping a cow to buy things? That's what normal people do.

Cows don't fit in your purse! 😄 All this new stuff is Roman, imported. They got a bad rep with the Gauls, but here we're all big Rome fanboys.

 Tsk, all this needless change. Next you'll be telling me these southern softies don't even bury their dead!

They do – but they burn them first! And then bury the ashes with way more treasure in the graves. Like pottery, mirrors, jars of wine, glass jewellery, chunky golden torcs! They've got loads of spare gold, so they're pretty chill about burying it!

 Spare gold? Why didn't you say that at the start?! I'm moving down south immediately – Granny's gonna get herself some bling!

SMELLS FISHY

Obviously no one was texting 2,000 years ago, but it's true that lots of new stuff arrived in southern Britain from northern Gaul (modern France). This included garum, which was like the ketchup of the ancient world – Romans put it on anything savoury. Remember, only Britons in the far north (modern Scotland) ate fish, so this would have been a very new flavour down south! Tweezers, make-up, mirrors and fancy jewellery worn around the neck, known as *torcs*, all appeared only in the south at this time. A real north/south divide!

Clearly, a lot is changing very quickly as Roman influence spreads here. But before we can sit back and enjoy a big slurp of rotten fish guts … are you seeing what I'm seeing? Over on the horizon, I'm sure I can see … ships? Lots of ships! There's definitely someone coming this way, and— UH-OH, IT'S THE ROMANS!!!

And their leader is the most famous Roman of them all…

4
CAESAR'S CHAOTIC CONQUEST CALAMITY

New timeline for a new era!

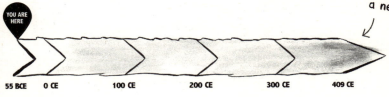

55 BCE   0 CE   100 CE   200 CE   300 CE   409 CE

Don't panic! I'm sure it's going to be fine... Oh no, look at the chaos meter – and the timeline has been updated for the new era of Roman Britain. Maybe we should panic a bit!

It's 55 BCE and storming his way across the narrow sea is trouble – BIG trouble. His name is Gaius Julius Caesar and he's only got one thing on his mind ... biscuits! Oops – no, that's me – I mean GLORY! Caesar has been leading a Roman rampage through Gaul, but now he's about to become the first ever Roman to head for British shores. Let's find out more about him...

We say Caesar like "Seezer", but in Latin his name was pronounced Guy-uss Yool-eeus Kye-sar.

— 27 —

FACT FILE: JULIUS CAESAR

Julius Caesar is a famous Roman politician from a very posh family, who is trying to make a name for himself by violently conquering the Gauls. Victory will let him return to Rome as a hero, with enough glory to grab the top political job (which will legally protect him from being punished for his horrible war crimes against the Gauls). Simple, right?

Annoyingly for Caesar, the Gauls don't seem too keen on being violently crushed and are fighting back. Caesar suspects they're getting help from the Britons, so he decides to do something about that. That means getting his sandals wet by crossing the Channel with 80 ships and a small army.

He was right – they definitely were!

Speaking of channels, imagine if Julius Caesar had been a YouTuber! It might have sounded a bit like this...

☰ JULIUS CAESAR LIVE!

@JuliusCaesarOfficial   Like Share Save

INVASION FOR BEGINNERS
Summer 55 BCE

Heyyyyy, welcome to Caesar's Conquest Cam! I'm Gaius Julius Caesar, Roman hero, military genius, descendant of the goddess Venus, and you're watching me conquering stuff live and loud – don't forget to like and subscribe! Today I'm going to show you how to squash the Gauls' allies in Britannia.

So, first off, I sent this fella called Commius ahead of me to tell the Britons to be chill when I arrive – smooth ol' J.C. does it again! Then I crossed the sea with my crack squad of troops – great lads, top bantz! The Britons must have had spies in my camp, cos they sent a big welcome party to greet us at the beach – although it wasn't much of a welcome, and definitely not a party! Nah, they tried to murder us as we got out of our boats. I guess my guy Commius failed to chill them out!

Obviously, when Britons are lobbing javelins at your head, most people would panic. Not me! We killed them all. IN YOUR FACE, BRITONS! And I took loads of hostages who I can kill if their families try to rebel against me. Ah, sweet Roman diplomacy, you gotta love it…

Caesar, OUT!

Well, that was easy! Although Commius was immediately arrested by the Britons, it doesn't matter. Caesar has successfully landed in Britain – or as the Romans call it, Britannia – and now he needs to establish a stronghold before moving inland. This will be easier than stealing sweets from a baby— OH, HANG ON!

☰ JULIUS CAESAR LIVE!

@JuliusCaesarOfficial

Like · Share · Save

THEY SAW IT COMING
Winter 55 BCE

Heyyyyy, so the Britons rebelled – NOT COOL! Also the stupid Britannia weather destroyed all my ships in a massive storm, so I'm stuck here … but that's fine! Totally fine! Obviously I crushed the rebellion, and I'll just have to build another navy. So while I wait for that, let's answer some questions from the comments section.

Comments

@TogaBoy88: What stuff have the Britons got? Can we steal it?

@JuliusCaesarOfficial: Thanks TogaBoy, great question. Yeah, it's mostly cows! Honestly, cattle just wander all over the place. What else? Uh … they've got loads of trees, and they mine for metals too – tin and iron, maybe some lead. They sometimes use iron weights instead of coins. Oh, and the cows are a type of cash, apparently! I guess you could call them *moo*-ney! Get it? Like *money*? Ha ha ha, top bantz!

@anonymous: What are the Britons like?

@JuliusCaesarOfficial: Well, remember those pesky Britons I suspected of meddling in Gaul? They're actually THE LEAST WORST ONES! I went further inland into Britannia. URGH! This place is dark and cold and wet, and I met the hordes of uncivilized violent barbarians who live there. And you won't believe what they look like! All the men grow these huge, gross moustaches on their top lips, yet they shave their bodies? That's the wrong way round, bro!!!

Also, during battle, they fight shirtless and paint themselves blue, instead of wearing armour – absolute weirdos! Admittedly it makes them fast runners, so they keep escaping from my soldiers, but it's just so RANDOM! Why wouldn't you want to wear heavy, noisy, brightly coloured armour? Wait, what's that rustling in the bushes? OH NO, THEY SNEAKED UP ON US AGAIN! GRAB YOUR SHIELDS, MEN: IT'S AN AMBUSH!

OK, that's it, I'm heading back to Gaul – but I'm not retreating! WHO SAID I WAS RETREATING?! HOW DARE YOU!!! No, this is a totally legit … er … *tactical* … um … *reconsolidation*, yeah? Because I'm a military genius. (Did I mention I'm descended from the goddess Venus?)

Caesar, OUT!

Looks like invading Britain isn't so easy after all! The Britons are fierce fighters – and all that (blue paint) sounds intimidating!

> The blue body paint is the famous image of the Britons – but Caesar was the ONLY person to mention this, and we have no archaeological evidence for it!

The Britons use their knowledge of the land to hide and then ambush the noisy Roman soldiers. Britain is also not a fun place to be in the cold, wet, dark winter – so Caesar legs it! But he's not gone for long. The following year it's time for *Caesar: The Sequel!*

Like most movie sequels, this invasion is bigger and better, as Caesar brings 800 ships, 20,000 soldiers and 2,000 horses with him and... WHOOPS! They've gone the wrong way! Yep, the navy has accidentally sailed right past Britain, and they're now having to row backwards.

The Caequel!

It's this way, guys!

Still, it's not a complete disaster: when they finally land, Caesar defeats ONE British leader, Cassivellaunus, in south-east England. So can we call this a successful invasion?

EPIC INVASION FAIL

I don't think anyone would call Caesar's invasions successful! He boasted about his double invasion of Britain in his famous book *Commentaries on the Gallic War*. But several Roman writers thought Caesar's British campaigns were a waste of time because it was just a random island on the edge of the map, and not worth conquering. Despite his boasting, Caesar achieved so little with his first invasion in 55 BCE, he had to pretend it was a research investigation! But even when he tried again in 54 BCE, and "conquered" what is now south-east England, he got no further north than the River Thames (modern London-ish) and soon had to leave again. People often think he said *Veni, vidi, vici* ("I came, I saw, I conquered") after his British adventure, but that was actually for a different war!

Oof, how embarrassing for Caesar – not only has he failed TWICE to conquer Britain, but his attacks have backfired by uniting many rival British groups against him. They used to hate each other, but now they have a common Roman foe! After that fiasco, surely the Romans will give up trying to invade for a while.

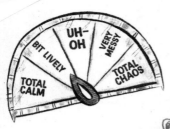

5

ROMAN INVASION 3: THIRD TIME'S A CHARM!

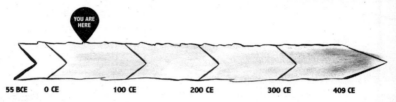

55 BCE 0 CE   100 CE   200 CE   300 CE   409 CE

Is that it for "Roman" Britain, then? What a disappointing washout! Here we are in 43 CE, nearly a hundred years after Caesar's double invasion attempt, and there's been no sign of them. But that's not to say things are boring around here. Having briefly joined forces against Caesar, the various British kingdoms are back to squabbling among themselves! Take a look at this map – there are lots of regional peoples ruled by different kings (and occasionally queens), all with different priorities. In fact, while some still hate Rome, others have become surprisingly pro-Roman. Hmm, that's gonna make things a bit complicated!

34

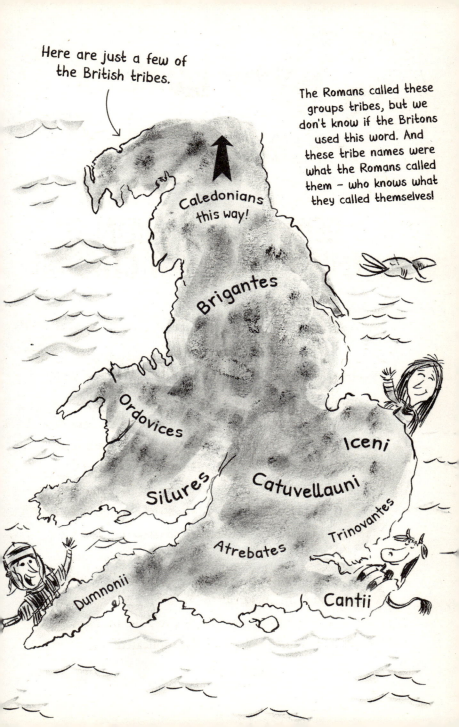

HAPPY FAMILIES

OK, DEEP BREATH… Do you remember Commius, whose job was to get the Britons to chill out before Julius Caesar arrived? Well, Commius created his own Atrebates kingdom in southern Britain, which is now being run by his son, Verica, who's having a tricky time. He is being bullied by two brothers (Caratacus and Togodumnus) from the powerful Catuvellauni kingdom. Their dad is King Cunobelinus – he's a big deal in the south-east corner of Britain, and it's not wise to mess with this family.

He was the first person in British history to put his face on a coin, something he copied off the Romans!

They ruled the lands north of modern London.

You might be thinking: "That doesn't sound complicated, Greg?", but just you wait! King Cunobelinus has a *third* son – Adminius – which is a lovely name that translates to "the gentle one". Aw, how sweet! Unfortunately he's not gentle at all! In fact, he's just ruthlessly conquered the Cantii people, only to then fall out with his father, who wants the Cantii lands for himself. And how has Adminius-the-not-very-gentle resolved this quarrel with daddy? By legging it to Rome to beg for help from the new emperor, Caligula! Hang on, though, what's an *emperor*?

The Cantii gave their name to Kent, where you grew up, Greg!

Caligula means "Little Boots" in Latin, because he was a tiny kid when he went to live with a Roman legion and became their mascot.

FACT FILE: ROMAN EMPERORS

Since 509 BCE, the Romans had banned kings and were ruled as a republic – the big decisions were made by rich politicians. However, the power-hungry Julius Caesar (yep, the failed invader) got around the ban by making himself "Dictator For Life" – definitely not a king (but still very much king-ish!). He was murdered, but the Roman Republic was not restored. Instead, Caesar's chosen heir – Octavian – became ruler over the whole Roman Empire, and was renamed Emperor Augustus. When he died, power passed to his stepson, Emperor Tiberius, whose grandson, Caligula, became Rome's third emperor in 37 CE.

OK, so here we are in the reign of Emperor Caligula, and King Cunobelinus – Adminius' scary dad – has been grumpily demanding Caligula sends his disloyal son back to Britain to be punished (and I don't think this means doing extra chores on the weekend...).

Emperor Caligula has three choices: send Adminius back to his furious dad, help Adminius invade Britain to retake his lands, or ignore them both. And Caligula chooses … INVADING BRITAIN!!!

SURPRISE ROMAN INVASION!

Yikes, it's happening again: the Romans are coming! Caligula is gathering troops on the shores of Gaul, and preparing the ships, and … oh, why is the chaos meter so calm?! Are the batteries dead?

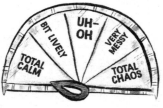

NO NEED TO PANIC!

False alarm, Greg! Emperor Caligula is famous in Roman history for behaving very strangely and cruelly. He allegedly gathered his army on the beach, but suddenly ordered his soldiers to collect seashells instead! So his invasion of Britain never happened, even though he <u>pretended</u> it did so he could throw himself a victory parade. Weird guy! Anyway, Adminius didn't get any Roman help, and we don't know what happened to him afterwards.

Oh, fair enough! I guess with Caligula preferring a lovely day trip to the seaside rather than a brutal invasion, that means Britain is safe?

But wait, I'm hearing Emperor Caligula has just been murdered for being such a horrible oddball! His replacement is Emperor Claudius, a very clever and nerdy emperor who loves writing (massively long history books.) ← He sounds like you and me, Greg! He's no muscular beefcake, and definitely not as obsessed with warfare as Julius Caesar, so now Britain surely MUST be safe?! I'm confident that's the end of the invasion chat, and—

VERICA NEEDS A FAVOUR

OOPS, SILLY ME, I FORGOT ABOUT VERICA!

I can hear you shouting: "Who is he again, Greg?" Fear not, Verica is the king getting bullied by those two Catuvellauni brothers, remember? Luckily for him, his dad (Commius!) worked with Caesar, and so Verica has called in some favours from his daddy's Roman friends. He's convinced Emperor Claudius to send a few troops to help protect his lands. Basically Verica is getting a bigger boy to help him fight his mean playground bullies, so when they say: "Oh, yeah?! You and whose army?!" he can say: "Me and *Rome's* army!" Great plan, this should definitely calm things down.

Here come the borrowed soldiers now…

Whoaaa! Hang on, that's not a *few* Roman troops –

THAT'S <u>20,000</u> LEGIONARIES!!!!

I didn't order this many!

We have no idea how Verica reacts to a huge army showing up on his doorstep, but I like to imagine him sending an awkward text to Claudius. Something like…

A Roman army legion contained between 4,000 and 6,000 soldiers.

Oh, um, hi, Emperor Claudius. Thanks for the soldiers. Just one thing: I ordered a small Roman battalion, but you seem to have sent FOUR legions?! Can I return some? Is there a 30-day refund period? It's just this looks a LOT like a Roman invasion force, and I wouldn't want the other British kings to blame me for accidentally inviting in a huge enemy army!

Hello, Emperor, did you get my message??

Yes, Emperor Claudius isn't doing Verica a favour – he's doing *himself* a favour! It seems Claudius – the book-loving nerd – is trying to outdo super-soldier Caesar by conquering Britain. What a shocker!

Claudius was very unpopular in Rome (they didn't like nerds: rude!) so he needed a great military victory to make his enemies stop trying to murder him.

ROMAN INVASION NUMBER 4: THEY REALLY, REALLY MEAN IT THIS TIME!

Imagine you're an ancient Briton from the Catuvellauni kingdom, and you're just minding your business – maybe milking your cows, or brushing your enormous bushy moustache (or even brushing milk out of your enormous bushy moustache) – when, out of nowhere, 20,000 legionaries arrive on your beach! You'd absolutely panic, wouldn't you? After all, it's been a hundred years since the last invasion, and nobody believed Verica when he said he was getting back-up! What are Togodumnus and Caratacus, those two big bully brothers from the Catuvellauni kingdom, going to do? Well, it seems Togodumnus quickly betrays his brother and switches to the Roman side – ooh, that's a bit cheeky! – so it's left to the new king, Caratacus, to lead his

legionaries were citizen soldiers of the Roman legions. There were also foreign auxiliary support troops.

Some historians think Togodumnus died in battle, but he probably switched sides and became known as Cogidubnus to the Romans.

people. By which I mean, lead them in running away!

And where do they run away to? The deep, dark forests, of course. Yep, the Claudian invasion of Britain basically begins with the Roman commander Aulus Plautius having to play a game of hide-and-seek with the Britons, who vanish into the trees like an army of moustachioed squirrels!

Eventually the Catuvellauni leave the forests and cross a big river, where they set up camp, thinking that there's no way the Romans can cross it in their heavy armour.

Wait, what are those Romans doing? Oh no! THE ROMANS HAVE ELITE FOREIGN SOLDIERS WHO CAN SWIM! It's total carnage, with the

The Romans recruited from all over their empire, and these German recruits were well trained in swimming and crossing marshlands.

shocked Britons cut down by sharp swords and pointy javelins – horrible!!!

The Catuvellauni survivors, and their other British allies, get chased all the way to the boggy marshland around the River Thames. At last they've made it to a safe place – even the mighty Julius Caesar got stuck here for months! The marshes are miserably cold and damp, and nobody – not even well-trained, mega-violent Roman legionaries with all their swimming badges – enjoys having wet socks and muddy underpants! Unable to advance, the Romans set up camp and wait. Meanwhile, General Plautius sends a letter back to Rome, and roughly three months later, guess who shows up in Britain?

It probably took five weeks for the letter to reach Rome.

TOOOOT TOOOOT!
It's only bloomin' EMPEROR CLAUDIUS himself!
TOOOOT!

Yes, Claudius needs a quick win to impress his army (and stop nerd-hating rivals murdering him!). Plus, Britain is apparently worth conquering because of its natural resources, so the emperor figures he should show up in person to get the job done!

THE EMPEROR STRIKES

WOW! Pity poor King Caratacus – he's already been betrayed by his brother, and now he's up against one of the most powerful rulers on the planet! I suppose at least it's a compliment that Claudius has travelled hundreds of miles to crush him in person. It's nice to be worth the hassle!

One Roman writer said that Claudius considered taking war elephants to Britain, but some historians don't believe this actually happened.

But, for Caratacus, it's obviously a disaster. Emperor Claudius quickly captures his capital town, Camulodunum, and sends messengers to all the other British kings, demanding they come and surrender to him in person. Imagine how shocked they must be to get this message – they've barely even *heard* of the Romans, let alone agreed to be ruled by them!

Modern Colchester.

Soon eleven confused and anxious British kings show up to accept Rome as their overlord, and that's pretty much mission accomplished for Emperor Claudius. Though Caratacus is still stubbornly resisting (as best he can without a capital), many other British rulers now kneel before Rome's mighty emperor. It took Julius Caesar nearly two years to invade only a small chunk of Britain, but Claudius has outperformed him in only sixteen days! This is why you've gotta watch out for book-loving nerds: they're the ones who get stuff done!

VERICA IS VERY, VERY SORRY

How is Verica feeling right now? Sure, he got his revenge over the Catuvellauni bullies, but it must be awkward when he bumps into those British kings who've been forced to submit to Rome because of him. Maybe he sent them an apology note? Imagine how that would sound...

> Hey, guys, so ... I think I might have accidentally got our island conquered – my bad! In my defence, when I asked for soldiers, I really thought they'd just give me money to hire my own, not send ACTUAL Romans! But I realize now that my actions were toxic, and I've hurt a lot of people and let my family down. I'm going to take some time to work on myself and grow as a person. (And also to drink this Roman stuff called wine – have you tried it? It's lovely!)
> With love, Verica x

So for many British kings, it's game over. But while Claudius claims to have conquered all of Britain, that's not true: Caratacus isn't giving up that easily...

6
JOIN THE RESISTANCE!

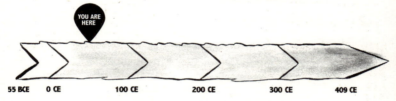

Since Claudius' invasion in 43 CE, the Romans have been battling their way across the southern half of Britain, taking control of towns and territory. Conquering the north will take much longer – those guys are not rolling over easily! Claudius has already gone home, having wallowed like a muddy hippo in his glory, so the day-to-day running of Rome's new → province has gone to Publius Ostorius Scapula, who has taken over from Plautius as governor of Britain.

A conquered region overseen by a Roman governor or magistrate.

Quickly Scapula sets about transforming Britain into a useful moneymaker for Rome, sending out engineers to build forts and roads, grabbing British grain to feed his soldiers, and forcing conquered Britons to mine precious metals that can be sent back to Rome. Some British leaders are playing along with the new system in return for generous payments, but not everyone is willing to sell out. For six years, King Caratacus has been fighting back. It's not been going well, and he keeps being forced further west, but now he's got a new plan! Shall we have a listen?

CARATACUS NEEDS YOU!

JOIN THE REBELS AND HELP DEFEAT THE EMPIRE

THEY'RE TAKING OUR HOMES!

THEY'RE KILLING OUR FAMILIES!

THEY'RE SENDING US DOWN MINES!

THEY'RE TAXING US!

THEY'RE CONFISCATING OUR SWORDS!

My fellow Britons, I – King Caratacus, leader of the British resistance – must speak truthfully. The Romans are winning.

But do not lose hope! We don't need to win battles; we just need to make them grow tired of fighting us. Caesar gave up, and we can make them abandon Britannia again. Let's move west – to the lands of our allies, the Silures and Ordovices – and sting the Romans like a million buzzing wasps!

Yes, Rome's armies are huge and well equipped. But they move slowly – let's attack with lightning speed! They wear colourful uniforms; we blend into the trees – let's ambush them, then vanish like ghosts! We know where their bases are, but they can't find ours – let's make them hunt for us, then make them regret it! Remember, we fight for our families; the Romans fight only for greed. They want to rule the whole world, but we don't have to agree to be ruled! Join the resistance, and WE <u>CAN</u> DEFEAT THE EMPIRE!

Oh … and if anyone has any Roman honey cakes, please bring them to my tent. The Romans might be evil, but they sure can bake!

GREEDY ROMANS

ACCURACY ALARM

Greg's imagined most of this speech, but various ancient sources confirm these were probably Caratacus' complaints and his plan. Also, "we fight for our families, the Romans fight only for greed" was a real quote by Caratacus, according to the Roman writer Tacitus. (Although Tacitus wasn't there at the time, so we don't know for sure!)

Powerful stuff! But it's no wonder Caratacus is angry. The Romans are building a temple dedicated to Emperor Claudius in Caratacus' former capital, while his soldiers burn the Britons' hill forts to the ground. The rebels are being forced to retreat <u>further west</u>, and are hearing horrible stories that the Romans are trying to wipe out the Britons' religion by targeting their religious leaders, the holy Druids. I guess a Druid is a kind of ancient priest?

Their allies were the Silures, in south-east Wales, and the Ordovices, in north Wales.

HOW TO SPOT A DRUID

ACCURACY ALARM

Actually a Druid was a mixture of philosopher, lawyer, priest and—

Sorry, Emma, I have to interrupt: BIG NEWS! The Romans have found Caratacus! He's deep in the heart of the western lands – but he *wants* to be found! He's laying a cunning trap by sitting high on a hill, protected by a gushing river on one side and big rocks on the other. The attacking Romans will be stuck between the unclimbable cliff and the unswimmable waters, while the Britons chuck javelins and rocks at them from higher up. It's a perfect plan, flawlessly executed, with nothing that can go wrong… Uh-oh!!!

DISASTER! Did I mention the Roman army has some very clever engineers? Yep, their finest carpentry boffins have banged out some temporary bridges, and – hey, presto! – the legionaries soon cross the river, swoop up the hill and smash into the British lines with stabby swords a-flailing! Run for your lives, Britons!

Caratacus and his family just about escape, ending up hundreds of miles away in northern Britain, at the court of Queen Cartimandua of the Brigantes people. Caratacus assumes she's on his side – surely all Britons hate Rome, right?

The Brigantes ruled over what is now Yorkshire.

WRONG! Cartimandua enjoys getting regular buckets of Roman cash, so she immediately hands Caratacus over. She gets a hefty reward, but it comes at a high price – her husband, Venutius, is so disappointed in her, he dumps her.

We'll come back to him later!

Oh dear! After nearly eight years of courageous resistance, poor Caratacus is about to be delivered to the Roman emperor in chains, like a hairy Christmas gift!

CARATACUS IN CHAINS

Unlucky Caratacus is carted off to Rome to be the star attraction in Claudius' victory parade, where the glitzy finale is meant to be Caratacus getting his head chopped off. It looks like Caratacus is about to come to a grisly end ... but what's this? Caratacus is suddenly launching into a passionate speech! Bit weird, but OK?

Yes, as he gazes out at the enormous crowd, Caratacus realizes that he has become really famous and feared in Rome! For the past eight years – while he's been getting cold and wet hiding in hill forts and bushes, caked in blood and mud – everyone in Rome has been gossiping about him as if he is the invincible British bogeyman. He realizes he can use that to his advantage!

Don't kill me, Emperor – I did you a favour! You needed glory, right? I gave you that!

I'm a terrifying barbarian who defied mighty Rome for eight years – you beat the best, which makes you the BESTEST best!

So why not let me go, huh? It would show you are merciful, and ensure the history books will talk about you for centuries to come!

Caratacus was right: here we are talking about it in a history book, nearly 2,000 years later!

Amazingly Caratacus' speech works! Remember, Claudius is a proper history buff, so the idea of being celebrated in future (history books) is very appealing to him! Incredibly, despite all the headaches he has caused, Caratacus and his family are released to become bewildered tourists, pootling around Rome and staring in amazement at the huge marble buildings that dwarf the damp, draughty roundhouses they left behind in Britain. What an unexpected end to the story!

Roman historian Tacitus wrote about all this in his book The Annals.

With Caratacus defeated, the British resistance is finished, right? Ah, well, no! Remember Venutius, former husband of Queen Cartimandua of the Brigantes, who dumped her because she betrayed Caratacus? Well, he's avenging Caratacus by becoming the new British rebel leader! And he's working closely with the Druids, who Emma was telling us about when I rudely interrupted her. Shall we try that again?

7

HOW TO SPOT A DRUID

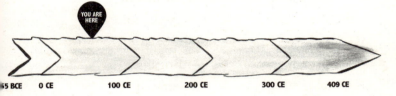

EMERGENCY UPDATE: Emperor Claudius is dead! His wife fed him poisonous mushrooms so her horrible teenage son, Nero, could rule as emperor instead. Nero has appointed a new British governor called Quintus Veranius, who is fighting the new rebel leader Venutius. So, our cast of characters has changed, but the plot of this movie remains the same – Rome versus the rebels!

Actually, not *entirely* the same. The Romans are now trying to kill off the religious leaders who inspire the rebels to keep fighting. These leaders are called Druids. Wanna know what a Druid does? Well, it depends who you ask…

WHAT IS A DRUID?

We asked Romans and Britons what they thought about the Druids. This is what they said!

ROMAN

"Druids are a terrifying mash-up of weirdo philosopher and murderous priest. They get very involved in war and politics – BE VERY SCARED! We hate them sooooo much!

BRITON

"Druids are important wise men. They remember our laws and history, and teach natural philosophy to young students. They also speak with the gods on people's behalf. Don't confuse Druids with Bards (who sing songs and compose poetry) and Vates (the priests who do religious sacrifices).

WHAT DO DRUIDS LOOK LIKE?

BRITON

"Uh ... just normal men with normal beards! I guess they are known for wearing long white robes and carrying an oak staff, if that's what you're asking?"

ROMAN

"EVIL WIZARDS! With long straggly beards, long white robes and a chunky oak staff. And they're covered in blood from all the human sacrifices they do!"

DO DRUIDS WRITE STUFF DOWN?

ROMAN

" No! They memorize everything, because the Britons are too barbaric to have written literature and laws, like us clever Romans.

BRITON

" Of course they do! Druids speak several languages, and have amazing memories. They write letters in Greek.

WHERE ARE DRUIDS FOUND?

ROMAN

" EVERYWHERE, JUST LIKE HORRIBLE BEARDY RATS! Julius Caesar saw them in both Gaul and Britannia. They're clearly part of a huge network stretching overseas, but our spies tell us the British Druids are the most important.

BRITON

" Druids used to be all over Britannia and in regular contact with their brothers in Gaul, but they have now been forced to retreat to the island of Mona, in the west, because of the aggressive Romans.

WHAT DO DRUIDS DO?

ROMAN

"Evil, creepy, weird stuff! When Caesar fought them, they muttered curses of dark magic to inspire the Britons. They claim they can tell the future by stabbing a man with a sword and seeing which way he falls! They worship oak trees. Caesar said they burned victims alive in giant sculptures made of wicker. Oh, and, if you think that's bad, Druids sometimes eat their sacrificial victims too – it's horrible stuff!

BRITON

"Druids are very busy! They act as judges for legal cases and also give top notch advice on what the gods are thinking. They study the cycle of the moon, and supervise the Vates during sacrifices. Plus they're philosophy teachers. Druids mainly teach about souls continuing to exist after death. It's good stuff!

Sometimes we do nothing...

GOODIES OR BADDIES?

It's hard to know the truth about Druids. The Romans made them sound monstrous, but people are rarely complimentary or honest about their enemies! We must be careful trusting some of these wild stories – but what if there was some truth to them? Ancient Roman writers said Druids performed fortune telling by sacrificing humans. Intriguingly, archaeologists found an ancient body in Lindow, north-west England, that had been stabbed AND strangled AND thrown into a bog, which some people think was a sacrifice. I think he was just murdered! Although Romans didn't regularly sacrifice humans, they happily killed them in the Colosseum for entertainment, and sacrificed animals to predict the future, so they were no saints either!

Well, there you have it – Druids are either slightly boring philosophers or violently magical maniacs! Either way, the Romans seem determined to get rid of them, so they're sending legions of soldiers to Mona to crush them, once and for all.

The island of Anglesey, off the north-west coast of Wales!

Yes, I think it's fair to say Claudius was fibbing when he claimed to have conquered Britain – clearly, there's loads of fighting still happening, fifteen years later. And actually, I think there may be a new type of trouble brewing over in eastern Britain, in the kingdom of Iceni. Let's go check it out!

BOUDICA BREAKOUT

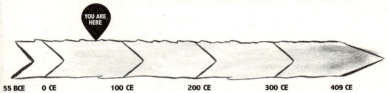

We've reached the year 60 CE. While the Romans are chasing Venutius through the green, green valleys of western Britain and hassling the Druids in Mona, over in eastern Britain there has been considerably less violence and screaming. Here, King Prasutagus – ruler of the Iceni people – has done a nice little deal with Rome. In return for staying loyal, the Iceni have mostly been left alone, and it's working great— OH DEAR, Prasutagus just died! Well, that's unfortunate, isn't it? Luckily he'd written a legal will to say that his daughters should rule after him – so it's no problemo!

Hmm, the chaos meter doesn't look so calm... I wonder why?

Cripes! Turns out we do have a problem – a HUGE, MASSIVE PROBLEMO! A Roman official named Catus Decianus just showed up to say the worst thing possible, worse even than saying: "I put a stinky dog poo in your sandwich!" Decianus said: "Hey, Iceni tribe, you know all that cash Emperor Claudius gave you to be loyal to Rome? It wasn't a gift … it was a loan. And now it's time to pay us back!" Yeah, that's going to annoy a bunch of people, isn't it? Particularly when they're grieving for their dead king! Even worse, Emperor Nero's personal teacher – a super-rich philosopher called Seneca – is also demanding payback for the cash he says he loaned to the Britons! That's two different bills the Romans are making them pay. This surely cannot get any worse?

HOW TO MAKE THINGS WORSE

It gets soooooo much worse! Decianus rips up Prasutagus' final will, and orders that the dead king's wife, Queen Boudica, should be brutally whipped and her daughters horribly attacked. It's a disgusting assault against innocent young women, and it all comes from the orders of the big-headed bully-boy Emperor Nero, who has decided the Iceni's lands should belong to him. Soon Roman soldiers are grabbing even more British land, and treating the shell-shocked Iceni like slaves.

Understandably Boudica and the Iceni are confused and furious – they're <u>CONFURIOUS!</u> How could the Romans be so sneaky and cruel?! Soon they are joined by their neighbours, the Trinovantes, whose capital town, Camulodunum, had previously been stolen by Caratacus' Catuvellauni family. When the Romans invaded, the Trinovantes assumed they'd get their town back. FAT CHANCE! The Romans turned Camulodunum into a retirement home for their soldiers, complete with a huge temple for Emperor Claudius. It's no wonder the Trinovantes are on Team Boudica!

Given all the terrible things they've done, you'd think the Romans might *expect* a British rebellion, right? After all, they're STILL fighting Venutius and the Druids in the west, so it's not as if the Britons have forgotten how to swing a sword! Yet the Romans seem clueless. Even when rumours spread of a possible British uprising, Camulodunum is left without ditches, ramparts or even enough soldiers to defend it. The Romans send only 200 random dudes, and they don't even have proper weapons!

Not a real word, Greg!

THIS is the best you can do?!

New research shows the Romans were so confident, they didn't have a single army fort in the entire south-eastern region of Britain!

Aaaaaand surprise, surprise, Queen Boudica has gathered a huge army and rebelled! It's total chaos – she's even knocked over our page numbers!

Boudica's rebels are furiously violent. They smash into Camulodunum, where hundreds of Romans are barricaded inside the Temple of Claudius, and Boudica shows them no mercy. After two days of Roman resistance, she storms the temple and horribly kills everyone inside – even women and kids! Then she burns everything down and heads off to Londinium ← Modern London! to do the same again… Can you believe the Romans didn't see this coming?

ACCURACY ALARM

SURPRISE!

Wait a second, Greg! The Romans didn't expect an attack because there were cunning British spies telling the Romans not to worry – while also secretly telling Boudica when to attack! The uprising wasn't random or spontaneous; it was a carefully organized revolution that was meant to catch the Romans with their pants down!

And that's not the only shock win for Boudica. Before reaching Londinium, Boudica's army wipes out 2,000 soldiers from the elite 9th Roman legion – only a few Roman soldiers escape to tell the terrible tale! ← It's one thing to overcome 200 random men in an unguarded town, but to take out 2,000 highly trained troops? That is a very bad sign for the Romans! Boudica knows what she is doing, and her army is growing in size as Britons flock to join her in getting revenge!

The 9th Legion suffered heavy losses, but managed to carry on fighting in Britain for another 60 years.

The news about the rebellion soon reaches the latest Roman governor of Britain – General Suetonius Paulinus – who is busy playing a violent game of slaughter-the-Druids on the western isle of Mona. Suetonius races back with his troops, but realizes it's too late to save Londinium. He can only evacuate some people, and retreat to find a battlefield that might give his small army a chance against the enormous British one.

Boudica continues doing her Godzilla impression, trashing Londinium and then heading north to Verulamium. → St Albans. She knows that if she can wipe out Governor Suetonius, Emperor Nero will pretty much have to give up on the island, and Britain will be free of Romans!

ACCURACY ALARM

TRASH TALK

You said Boudica trashed three towns – Camulodunum, Londinium and Verulamium – as this is what the Roman writer Tacitus says. But modern archaeology suggests the Roman towns of Calleva Atrebatum (Silchester), Caesaromagus (Chelmsford) and Ad Pontes (Staines) were also burned at this time! Why didn't ancient writers mention them? Maybe they were pretending the revolt wasn't a big deal? Or maybe they just weren't paying attention properly?!

OK, so maybe Boudica smashes up six towns! Which might explain why she is super confident about the upcoming battle with Suetonius. After all, by this point she has an army of 70,000 angry warriors who absolutely hate the cruel Romans and their taxes, whereas Suetonius has only cobbled together a ragtag assortment of 10,000 Romans. He's meant to have 20,000, but the 9th Legion is still battered, bruised and bandaged from losing to Boudica the first time around, and the commander of the 2nd Legion is so terrified, he refuses to leave his fort!

Yep, they hid behind their walls in Exeter!

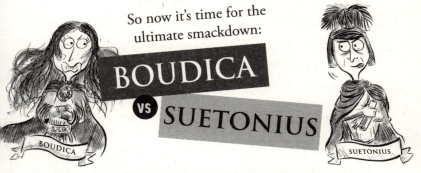

So now it's time for the ultimate smackdown:

BOUDICA vs SUETONIUS

BOUDICA

SUETONIUS

LET BATTLE COMMENCE!

Boudica rolls up to the battlefield and gives an inspirational speech to her warriors. They're so confident, they've brought thousands of family and friends, who park their carts behind the British troops so they can watch the slaughter with a picnic, like it's a delightful cricket match! But the Britons have forgotten two important things...

Historians call this the Battle of Watling Street, but there's loads of disagreement about where that actually was!

1. The heavily armoured Romans are brilliant fighters, with big shields and tactical discipline.
2. Suetonius has chosen this battlefield for a very good reason!

As the Britons charge forward, they realize they are being funnelled into a narrow valley with trees to the left and right of them. Even though they outnumber the enemy 7 to 1, the trees prevent them from spreading out, or sweeping behind the Romans. Instead Boudica's troops are like a horde of impatient train passengers squeezing through a carriage door! The warriors in the second and third rows are tripped and trampled by their overeager pals pushing from behind. Meanwhile, the Romans mercilessly stab the unarmoured Britons squished at the front … oh, the humanity!

These numbers might be big exaggerations from Roman historians.

Suddenly the Britons realize they're being annihilated! They try to run away, but they can't escape the funnel of doom because all their picnicking pals are blocking their path – the army has been trapped by its own cheerleaders! The Romans advance like murderous robots, cutting down the panicking Britons. By the end of day, tens of thousands lie dead on the ground, but only 400 of them are Roman!

Well, that's what the Romans said, anyway – not sure we can trust them!

Totally defeated, Boudica vanishes. Some say she drinks poison to avoid the Romans parading her in chains, like they did with Caratacus. Others say she dies of disease. Either way, her rebellion has failed – and the Romans immediately double down on building defensive forts to ensure it doesn't happen again.

ROMAN BRITAIN IS HERE TO STAY

Phew, what a story! Although … some historians – like Emma! – would argue that we can't be sure it's totally true. After all, the Roman sources we have don't always match up, and we don't have any British ones. In fact, there's quite a lot to debate here! *Bring it on!* Which means it's time to cue the music and moody studio lights for…

HISTORIAN HEAD-TO-HEAD

Two historians, two different theories: who will be the winner? Let's get ready to rumble!

Greg

Emma

ROUND 1
WHAT DO WE REALLY KNOW ABOUT BOUDICA?

Everyone knows what Boudica looked like! In movies, people always give Boudica long, wavy red hair. However, Dio Cassius, a Roman writer, said her hair was "xanthotatos" (the ancient Greek word for "very golden"), so I think she was more blonde than ginger. He also said she was very tall, wore a colourful tunic and a thick cloak fastened with a brooch.

Sorry, Greg, but Dio Cassius never even met her! He makes her sound like a roaring lioness, perhaps to show how beastly she was to his fellow Romans. Dio's Boudica is described as having her hair down, because Romans thought this was a sign of uncivilized manliness, so it makes her sound like a horrible barbarian. Also, they thought that all Britons were blonde!

OK, so maybe we don't know her hair colour. But surely Boudica was real, otherwise who burned down all those towns?!

Well, yes, but we don't know for sure if Boudica was her actual name! Some think that Boudica meant "victory" in her ancient language, so maybe it was an honorary title given to her after she destroyed Camulodunum? Maybe her real name was ... er ... Susan?!

But the rebellion definitely happened! Archaeologists have found the burned ashes from those destroyed towns, and immediately after 61 CE there was a famine and a reduction in taxes collected. Why? Because so many had died, and there were not enough people to harvest the crops. This rebellion definitely wasn't a made-up story, so at least we agree that Boudica was a real person.

ROUND 2
WHICH ANCIENT ROMAN HISTORIAN IS MOST TRUSTWORTHY?

We have two main sources: Dio Cassius lived over a century after the rebellion, whereas Tacitus was alive at the time. In fact, Tacitus married the daughter of a famous Roman governor of Britain – Gnaeus Julius Agricola – who was an eyewitness to Boudica's rebellion! That makes Tacitus more trustworthy, I think. He probably heard war stories from his father-in-law, and wrote them down!

Maaaaaybe... Tacitus was a little toddler during the revolt, and his stories told decades later might be exaggerated or misremembered!

But why would Tacitus write about Boudica if he didn't know his stuff? He was one of the greatest historians of the ancient world!

That's the interesting thing: Tacitus's book wasn't really about Boudica at all — it was about various Roman emperors, and he wanted to make Nero look terrible! In fact, Tacitus makes Boudica being dishonoured and whipped sound very similar to the famous Roman legend of Lucretia, who was a woman attacked by the son of a horrible Roman king, Tarquinius. Lucretia's tragic death caused the Romans to ban kings. I think Tacitus uses Boudica's story to remind everyone that Nero was just like the hated Tarquinius!

Even if Tacitus got creative in reshaping Boudica's story to sound like a legend Romans already knew, I still trust him more than Dio Cassius. Dio only knew about two towns being burned, and never mentioned Boudica wiping out the 9th Legion! That's key info to get wrong, no?

Yes, that's fair, but Tacitus also missed out things. He only mentions three towns being burned, but archaeology tells us it was at least six. I'm not sure we can trust either of them!

Really?! I think both historians give us great detail, which feels true to me. Tacitus makes Boudica so brave before battle, and Dio reports her speech about the Britons being victims of cruel Roman cheating. These speeches tell a story that I think is believable!

Nope, Boudica didn't say those actual words: Tacitus and Dio Cassius imagined them for her, to support their own political views. Even though they make her an impressive warrior, and we feel sympathy for how she was wronged, Boudica is still described by both men as a wild, unladylike, horrible barbarian — that's the Romans for you; they can't help themselves!

Hmm, it's such a shame we don't have any sources by ancient Britons to challenge these untrustworthy Roman writers. But I still prefer Tacitus to Dio Cassius!

AND THE WINNER IS...

NO ONE

Even I can't quite remember what I said.

That's right – it's great to ask questions, but we don't always have the answers. Our big debate shows we should be careful trusting Roman sources – sometimes people were writing stories to entertain, or to make a political point, and sometimes they just got things wrong because they weren't there. Sadly, we don't have Boudica's version of events.

Anyway, we're not even halfway through the book yet, so ONWARDS WE MARCH! Boudica is defeated, the Romans control half of Britain, and even Venutius has given up on rebelling (for now, at least!). At last the Romans can start making their mark.

Though not the west or the far north...

He tried again a few years later!

In fact, the most pressing matter is repairing Britain's smouldering towns after Boudica's uprising. Let's check out the building work, shall we? Actually, are you good at bricklaying? Perhaps you can lend a hand!

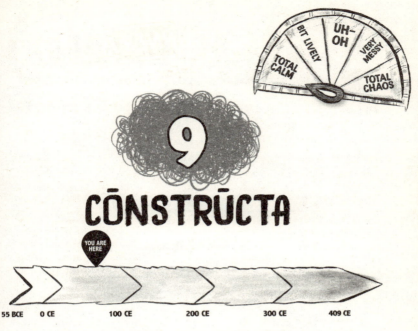

9
CŌNSTRŪCTA

After all that drama, Britain is now an orderly province of the Roman Empire, and after spending twenty years bringing it under control, it's time the Romans started making the place look ... well, more Roman! That involves building new forts, converting British towns into Roman ones, and even building brand-new settlements. Which means it's time to play *Cōnstrūcta*, the video game that lets you build a Roman town! Ready? Click PLAY!

CŌNSTRŪCTA

First, choose which type of town to build:

VICUS
A small village near a Roman fort that sells stuff to the soldiers.

CANABA
Like a vicus, but medium-sized.

CIVITAS
The busiest market town in a region, acting as the new capital for a conquered British tribe.

MUNICIPIUM
A large town for Roman citizens and some Britons. Allowed to make its own local laws.

COLONIA
The fanciest town for Roman citizens. Converted forts for retired soldiers and their families.

You have chosen civitas!
Do you want to knock down the existing British town and start over, or add to it?

ADD TO IT

> DEFENCES

You've already got some buildings, so place defensive ditches around the outside of your square-shaped town. Don't worry about defensive walls; those are expensive – they can wait a couple of hundred years.

> ROAD-BUILDING FOR NEWBIES

You'll need to connect your town to other places, so traders (and armies!) can get there easily. Roman roads are amazing engineering feats that can go in a straight line for hundreds of miles. Remember they need to be *cambered* with a gentle hump, so rainwater runs into the side gutters, and with raised *crepido* walkways either side. Include signposts and mile markers to help travellers find their way.

Congratulations, you have built your first Roman road!

Now criss-cross your town with narrower streets, marked out on a grid system. This will create a chequerboard of squares where you can put buildings!

CŌNSTRŪCTA

> BASILICA BUILDER

Every Roman town needs a forum – this is the place for speeches, trials, voting, tax collection, entertainment and shopping. Make a big courtyard, with covered walkways (called porticoes) round the sides. On the fourth side, build a huge multi-storey basilica, with a platform for speech-making. You'll also need temples, a curia (council chamber) for debating laws, a library, archives, plenty of statues, shops and fast-food joints. This place needs to feel busy!

> HYGIENE HELPER

URGH, what's that stench?! It seems Britons aren't as cleanliness-obsessed as Romans. Quick, build a *thermae* bathhouse, before people pass out from the stink! Remember, thermae need an underfloor *hypocaust* furnace to heat the bathwater above. They also have tepid rooms, indoor and outdoor swimming pools, a chilly plunge pool and a gym.

> FLOW FAIL ALERT!

Oh dear, your thermae isn't working because you haven't connected it to a water system! You need to bring water into the town with long channels linked to local springs and wells. Cheap wooden pipes will do if you can't afford massive stone-built aqueducts like the ones in Rome.

> BOGS BUDDY

No Roman town is complete without public toilets (foricae) and the sewers below them to catch the yucky emptying of bladders and bowels! Dig an underground channel to drain this sewage away. And why not install wooden or stone gutters in your streets to carry away rainwater? It rains a lot in Britannia and you don't want slippery pavements!

CŌNSTRŪCTA

> HOUSE-BUILDING HELPER

Time to build some houses! Put the fancy stone and brick homes near the forum. Poor people can live in wooden houses near the town's boundaries. Remember to build craft workshops, bakeries, forges, pottery and glass-blowing factories, and other handy wooden shacks for ordinary people to do their jobs in.

> RAZZLE-DAZZLE RECOMMENDER!

Town life should be fun! Romans love music, theatre, chariot races and gladiator fights – but these all require different venues, so choose wisely. A circus is a hairpin-shaped chariot track, or there's a semicircular theatre for plays, or a circular amphitheatre for gladiator combat. These are all huge, so put them on the edge of town. They're also expensive – start with wooden ones before splurging on a stone upgrade!

Your town is ready to go – great job!

As you can see, these new Roman towns are pretty impressive! And the Romans sure built a lot of them: in fact, if you live in a town in Britain today whose name ends in -caster, -chester or -cester, then it was originally a Roman fort.

> Between 50 and 70 CE, lots of new towns were founded, including what we now call Exeter, Leicester, Southampton, Cambridge, York, Winchester, Carlisle, Bath and Silchester.

Although maybe you're not sure if you'd like to live somewhere with pongy foricae toilets?! Well, the Romans are actually very concerned with hygiene and health: when someone dies, they bury them OUTSIDE the town, near the main road, to stop disease spreading. Sometimes they cremate (burn) the remains instead. And when anyone gets sick, they can go to the temple for a cure from the gods!

Talking of gods, that's another important way the Romans are starting to change Britain. Let's find out more!

10

GOD SWAP!

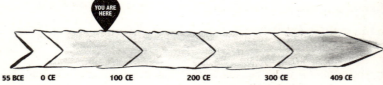

55 BCE   0 CE   100 CE   200 CE   300 CE   409 CE

As well as plonking new towns and roads all over the place, the Romans are also introducing Britons to Roman ways of worship. Normally, meddling in people's religion is a huge trigger for rebellion, but the chaos meter is doing fine, so I guess this idea isn't so unpopular! That's a nice surprise, for once...

Obviously there have been some teensy teething problems with religion recently, what with the Romans obsessively killing the sacred Druids. But now they are pitching a different approach – a big switch-over to their polytheistic faith, but with plenty of compromise! How they launch this idea to the Britons, we don't really know. The Britons can't read, so maybe someone makes a big announcement?

Polytheistic means more than one god. Britons were also polytheistic, but their gods had different names.

⇐ 80 ⇒

Dear conquered Briton,

You may have noticed some changes in your local religious centre. Do not be alarmed! We – the Roman government – are introducing upgrades following your recent murderous rebellion. We have listened, we have learned, and we're determined to be the all-conquering superpower who cares. We want what you want (so long as what *you* want is what we want…).

We will soon be updating religious customs in Britannia – but rest assured that we SHALL NOT BAN your beloved gods. In fact, we've realized they are much like our own! You're welcome to enjoy your original British gods, swap to our Roman ones (we have twelve major gods, and thousands of minor ones), or you can even combine their names to create new Romano-British gods – have fun with it!

Our new fleet of Roman priests will help you get to grips with our way of worship. Don't worry, we think you will enjoy these new changes. And please, don't burn down any more temples!

Yours faithfully,
Marcus Trebellius Maximus, Governor of Britannia

The Britons and the Romans worship many similar gods, which should help the religious switch-over go pretty smoothly. Not all British gods have Roman equivalents – but if in doubt, Britons can just worship Mars. He's the Roman god of war, but the Britons apparently decide he's the god of pretty much *everything*! Check out this handy guide to the Romano-British god universe…

The Britons associated Mars with 35 different gods – including the gods of healing, peace and plentiful food. He was the most popular Roman god by far!

MEET THE GOD SQUAD

BRITISH NAME	GODLY JOB	IS THERE A ROMAN VERSION?	IS THERE A ROMANO-BRITISH NAME?
Toutatis	God of the tribe	Mars/Apollo/Mercury	Mars Toutatis
Cernunnos	Horned god of nature	No	No
Epona	Goddess of horses	No	No
Belenus	God of healing	Apollo	Belenus Apollo
Sulis	Goddess of healing springs	Minerva	Sulis Minerva
Nodens	God of healing	Mars	Mars Nodens
Taranis	God of thunder	Jupiter	Jupiter Taranis
Maponos	God of youth	Apollo	Manopus Apollo
Viradecthis	Goddess of childbirth	Lucina	No

HOW TO WORSHIP

It's not just the gods that are open to collaboration. Instead of rolling out their usual temple-building programme, where stuff looks the same everywhere in the empire, here in Britain the Romans are allowing a new style of Romano-British temple that blends both traditions, and sits on holy sites the Britons already use. Britons consider rivers and springs to be sacred, so the Romans build special sanctuaries at these sites, like the impressive bathhouse and healing temple at Aquae Sulis. ← Modern Bath, in Somerset.

They also allow Britons to continue sacrificing dogs at their healing sanctuaries – sorry, dogs! However, they politely ask Britons to stop sacrificing humans. After all, killing people is wrong, and Romans are 100% opposed to it, AT ALL TIMES! (Unless it's during a battle, or in a gladiatorial arena, or if the victim is enslaved, or if someone harms the emperor, or murders their dad, or if someone damages crops, or …well, you get the picture.)

One potentially awkward situation is that the Romans think their emperors are descended from gods, but the Britons HATE the idea of worshipping real people. As a compromise, the Romans demand that twice a year – on 3 January and on the anniversary of the emperor's coronation – citizens must give offerings to both the emperor and Jupiter, but it's fine not to for the rest of the year. How flexible of them!

TALKING TO THE GODS

While the Britons can no longer consult local Druids and Vates (because they're mostly dead!), they can now speak directly with their chosen god, provided they make an offering. A typical gift to a god includes coins, small pots, jewellery, miniature figurines, sculptures of injured body parts, meat, sacrificed animals or blood.

They can also offer up a handmade votive plaque. These are flat, beautifully decorated slices of lead or silver with the god shown in the middle, and then space to write a promise or vow saying you'll do something in return for the god's help.

> One of the biggest changes the Romans brought was the idea of writing religious things down on metal and stone so they'd last for ever.

People can also ask the gods to get revenge on someone who has wronged them by using a curse tablet! Don't know what curse to ask for? Here are some great examples:

> LET THE MAN WHO STOLE MY RING, AND ANYONE WHO HELPED HIM, BE CURSED IN HIS BLOOD AND HIS EYES AND ALL HIS LIMBS AND LET EVEN HIS GUTS ROT AWAY! HE IS DONE FOR!

> SOLINUS ASKS SULIS MINERVA TO STOP THOSE WHO HAVE DONE ME WRONG FROM SLEEPING, AND TO TAKE AWAY THEIR HEALTH!
> I DON'T CARE WHETHER THEY ARE MALE OR FEMALE, ENSLAVED OR FREE, UNTIL THEY GIVE MY STUFF BACK.

> DOCIMEDIS HAS LOST TWO GLOVES AND WANTS THE PERSON WHO STOLE THEM TO GO MAD AND HAVE THEIR EYES FALL OUT IN MINERVA'S TEMPLE.

> These real curses are just 3 of the 130 tablets found at Aquae Sulis.

The cursing idea sounds so much fun – no wonder Britons accepted this new way of doing religion. Who doesn't want to cast spells on their enemies?!

> **ACCURACY ALARM** — **OH MY GODS!** BEEEEEEEP! BEEEEEEEP!
>
> Surprisingly, it does seem that Britons were very accepting of these religious changes – although we don't know why! In fairness, the Romans were very used to doing this – each conquered country got its own cast of Roman + local fusion gods, unique to them. So, for example, Sulis Minerva was only worshipped in Britain. Interpretatio Romana is the name of the system for giving Roman names to foreign gods who seem to do the same job.

Yep, this is a pretty smooth religious switch-over – isn't it nice to have a bit of peace and quiet? Although come to think of it, we haven't checked in on western Britain in a while. Let's go and take a peek. Be warned, I think we might be wading back into chaos…

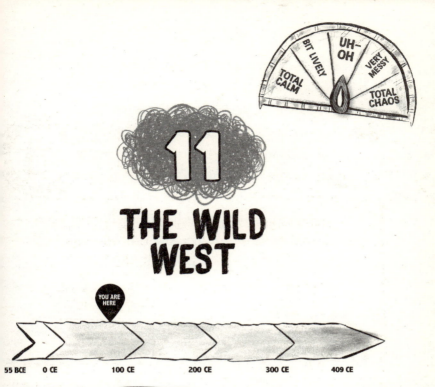

11
THE WILD WEST

Ah, beautiful (western Britain), with its soaring hills and lush green valleys. It's a truly lovely bit of countryside, but the Romans haven't had chance to enjoy picturesque picnics or invigorating riverside walks, because they've spent all their time here battling with Caratacus and Venutius and their scrap-happy western allies, the Silures and Ordovices. Since Caratacus was captured in 50 CE, there have been NINE Roman governors who've tried different strategies to handle these impressively stubborn rebels. Some hid behind defensive walls, some tried to ignore the enemy, one tried

This region is now the nation of Wales/Cymru, but the Romans just called it Britannia.

Fearsome Welsh warriors who gave the Romans big problems for over 30 years.

peaceful negotiation, and some went into all-out attack mode (and lost!).

Eboracum is now called York. The Caledonians were in Scotland.

All the while, throughout the 70s CE, the Romans have also been pushing northwards, building a big fort at Eboracum, fighting the Brigantes and venturing all the way up into Caledonia for messy punch-ups! But every time they head north, the western rebels refuse to behave themselves and they're forced to divert their attention.

So here we are in the year 80 CE, with a new governor – Gnaeus Julius Agricola – and he is determined to end this resistance for good!

The father-in-law of the historian Tacitus, who told Boudica's story!

FACT FILE: JULIUS AGRICOLA

Agricola is a warrior with a very impressive report card. Not only has he got political experience in both Rome and West Asia, but – aged 21 – he fought alongside Governor Suetonius in his famous victory against Boudica. So Agricola knows Britain, knows the Britons and knows how to win! He's just conquered the Brigantes in the north – could western Britain be next?

Here comes Agricola: ooh, and he's taken out the Ordovices – BOSH! He's gone after the remaining Druids on the island of Mona – WHACK! And he's squishing the Silures – SPLAT! Yes, a mere 37 years since the Roman conquest began, Agricola has finished what so many other governors couldn't: western Britain is *finally* Roman.

STRESSED ABOUT THE WEST

This means it's time to build the stuff needed to *keep* western Britain Roman! You see, the Romans may have won, but they are still terrified of *another* rebellion.

So, they plonk three legions (with 5,000 soldiers in each) into three forts at Viriconium Cornoviorum, Deva Victrix and Isca. These forts perch on the eastern edge of the newly conquered lands, meaning the troops can race off in any direction if needed. The Romans also dump 35 auxiliary regiments into smaller forts dotted all over western Britain. Basically, there are Roman soldiers EVERYWHERE. Pop your

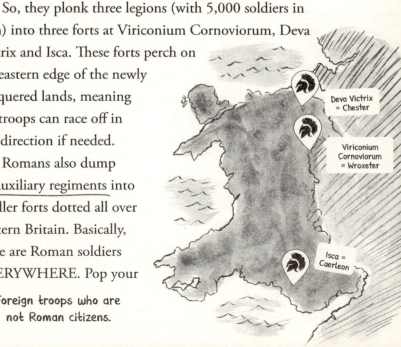

Deva Victrix = Chester

Viriconium Cornoviorum = Wroxeter

Isca = Caerleon

Foreign troops who are not Roman citizens.

head in any random hedge and you'll probably find one having a wee!

Feeding all these men requires 7,300 tonnes of wheat every year, grown on a stonkingly massive 21,000 acres of farmland, which means many more farmhouses need to be built. If you don't know what an (acre) is, don't worry – neither do I!

An acre is about the size of half a football pitch!

ALL CHANGE IN THE WEST

Swords are back in their sheaths, and western Britain is rapidly and radically changing, and becoming like the other conquered parts of Britain. Rich Romans are claiming ownership of common land, which forces British farmers to drive their cows to new feeding places further away. It's a bad time for cows … in fact, it's a terrible time, because Roman soldiers use cows for target practice – horrible!

Bull's eye!

Actually, I think you hit its bottom.

Yep, we have found bolts, shot from giant crossbows embedded in cow skulls!

Just like in the rest of
Britain, people in the newly
conquered west are eating more
sheep, deer, chicken, duck and
– at long last – oysters, shellfish
and fish. There are also many
new fruits and veggies – apples,
pears, sloes, blackberries,
grapes, figs, cherries, plums,
walnuts, dill, celery and olives. Much healthier! The
Romans also introduce rabbits and rats to Britain.

I can't believe I didn't try this before!

Sort of! Unfortunately these sweet new foods made people's teeth much less healthy!

It's not just the food that's changing in western
Britain. Coins finally arrive, 200 years after first
being used in southern Britain, and new types
of pottery, jewellery and fabric are also arriving
from abroad. Rich people are buying imported candles
and ceramic oil lamps to light their rooms, and they're
putting locks on their front doors and jewellery boxes –
clearly, they don't want their nice new stuff to be stolen!

Oh, and houses are changing too! In the southern
lands of the conquered Silures, roundhouses are going
square, and new villages are popping up. Just like in the
rest of Britain, old army forts are being converted into
towns for retired Roman soldiers to mingle
with the locals, get married, learn each other's
languages, and have Romano-British kids.
In the countryside, newly rich farmers are

The forts at Moridunum and Venta Silurum became big towns (modern-day Carmarthen and Caerwent).

building themselves fancy villas with tiled roofs, baths, gardens, pretty mosaic floors and snazzy ornaments. Everything is going a bit posh!

All this suggests everything is calm in Britain…

YEAH, RIGHT, have you forgotten the name of this book?! Nah, the west might finally be conquered, but things are still pretty tense at the northern edge of the Roman Empire, where foreign auxiliary soldiers are on guard at Vindolanda Fort. Shall we go and see how they're getting on?

Archaeologists have discovered 29 Roman villas in Wales, often linked to busy farms or iron production.

12
LIVING ON THE EDGE

YOU ARE HERE

55 BCE — 0 CE — 100 CE — 200 CE — 300 CE — 409 CE

The only unconquered area of mainland Great Britain is now Caledonia, in the northernmost part of the island. But, boy oh boy, the Romans sure would love to conquer it! In order to do so, they need a military base close to Caledonia, so they've built loads of forts in northern Britain. The best known one is called Vindolanda, hosting a thousand auxiliaries from other parts of the empire, most notably Batavia. These soldiers have all signed up for 25 years in the army, after which they'll be made Roman citizens. But it's dangerous, discipline is harsh, and the punishment for running away is sometimes death! Would you fancy signing up?

You can visit Vindolanda Fort in Northumbria — it's great!

This region is now part of the Netherlands.

What do you reckon – could you live here with only ditches and three-metre-high ramparts to keep those scary Caledonians at bay? You'd mainly be eating bread, bacon and cheese, though you can always buy extra stuff from the <u>vicus</u> outside. And if you think it's bad sharing a bedroom with a smelly brother, imagine sharing a barracks with 79 other soldiers! It's not all bad: soldiers play board games and dice, exercise together (boxing is a big favourite), sew and have a rota for chores. Still, it's cushier to be a (centurion), who sleep in their own spacious houses. Even better, the camp commander, Flavius Cerialis, gets a huge villa with his own private garden ... sweeeeet!

A vicus was a village that popped up next to forts to sell stuff to soldiers.

Centurions were junior officers in charge of 80 men.

Roman legionaries <u>can't marry until after they retire</u>, but foreign auxiliaries can bring their wives and kids along. You could be sharing a room with screaming toddlers! It could be worse: Vindolanda's horse-riding cavalry troops have to sleep next to their horses. What a night*mare*!

This rule was often ignored: archaeologists found the tombstone of centurion Vivius Marcianus, which was set up by his wife!

The main thing you'll notice, however, is how many rules there are. And how much incredible organization it takes to keep everyone fed, clothed and paid. People are writing lots of stuff down to keep track of it all – what a shame none of this will survive for historians to read!

VINDOLANDA TABLETS

BEEEEEEEP! **ACCURACY ALARM**

Don't worry, Greg: 1,700 documents from the fort survived to the present day! The Vindolanda Tablets are an amazing collection of messages written in ink on postcard-sized pieces of thin wood. They date back to 90-100 CE, but they were only discovered in the 1970s! These tablets are famous because they reveal so much about the organization of a Roman fort – but they also show normal life. We can see people asking for days off, requesting more socks, and even an invitation to a birthday party! It's incredible luck they survived, because wood normally rots (fortunately Vindolanda has fantastic *anaerobic* soil conditions) and also because Roman soldiers tried to burn them when they abandoned the camp. By pure chance, the fires went out, so the tablets survived – maybe we can thank the famous Britannia rain for this historical miracle!

Wow! What an amazing discovery to reveal life at the northern edge of the Roman Empire. But the Romans don't want this to stay as the edge – they want to conquer Caledonia too! Will they do it? Let's find out...

13
HADRIAN'S WALL

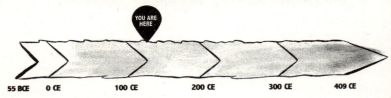

Despite having a mightily impressive fort up north in Vindolanda, the Romans are facing a problem in their plan to expand the empire further – they have run out of conquering juice!

Actually, that's not true. What's really happened is they have bumped into the Caledonians, who have no intention of becoming Romans: they like their own language, they like their own roundhouses (and brochs, if you go even further north), and they like their own foods. No amount of juicy olives or tangy garum sauce will convince these Caledonians to surrender their independence, and so they're putting up one hell of a fight!

Not even mighty military maestro Governor

The Caledones were the largest group in ancient Scotland, but the Romans also listed eight others: Venicones, Damnonii, Vacomagi, Taexali, Epidii, Votadini, Novantae and Selgovae.

Agricola was able to vanquish them, and vanquishing was very much his speciality! (He conquered western Britain, remember?) Sure, he won big time at the Battle of Mons Graupius in 83 CE, and he did his best to rampage around northern and western Caledonia, trashing whatever he could trash, building loads of forts, and strangling the enemy's supply network.

We have no idea where this famous battle was fought — there are loads of different theories!

But did it work? Naaahhh! Agricola found himself chasing a clever enemy who kept vanishing, only to pop up somewhere else with a surprise ambush, making the Roman invasion of Caledonia feel more like a frustrating game of whack-a-mole! Agricola eventually gave up and went home.

Since then, Britain has had EIGHT different governors, none of whom have made better progress. Clearly, Operation Crush Caledonia isn't working, so it's time for a new plan!

EMPEROR HADRIAN'S BIG IDEA

Fear not! We've reached 122 CE, and here comes a new Roman emperor, Hadrian, with some bold new thinking. He's going to build a MASSIVE wall, running from east to west, and plonk it three-fifths of the way up the island of Britain (just north of Vindolanda Fort). It's going to take three Romans legions (that's 15,000 men) at least six years to build it, and it'll cost a fortune to maintain, but hopefully this will stop the Caledonians attacking Roman Britain!

Maybe ten years!

ACCURACY ALARM — Sorry to interrupt, Greg, but we're not sure that's what it was for!

Oh? OK, so ... they're building a massive wall to mark the edge of the Roman Empire, and—

> Well, it's a bit more complicated than that!

Ooh, I know... it's designed to prevent giant robot hamsters from attacking major cities!

> Definitely not, Greg!

Hmm, this is harder than I thought! Seems like there's a lot of myths around Hadrian's Wall. Emma, why don't you take over, and help us separate the facts from the fiction?

> OK!

14

MYTH BUSTER: HADRIAN'S WALL SPECIAL!

HADRIAN'S WALL WAS 80 MILES LONG, 6 METRES HIGH AND 4 METRES THICK

Not quite! Hadrian's Wall — which the Romans called *Vallum Aelium* — was 80 *Roman* miles, but their miles were shorter than ours, so it's actually 73 miles long. The wall was 4.5 metres tall, and mostly 2.4 metres thick. It was meant to be thicker, but the plans changed halfway through. Originally, 49 (Roman) miles of wall were built in stone and 31 miles in grassy turf, with a mini fort every mile, and a watchtower every 500 metres.

MYTH BUSTER 2

HADRIAN'S WALL WAS THE BORDER BETWEEN ENGLAND AND SCOTLAND

Nope! England and Scotland didn't even exist at the time, and today the wall is far south of Scotland's border, running from Wallsend (near Newcastle) to Bowness-on-Solway (near Carlisle) in England.

HADRIAN'S WALL WAS THE NORTHERNMOST POINT OF THE ROMAN EMPIRE

Nope again! In 142 CE, Emperor Hadrian's successor Antoninus Pius built a second wall about 100 miles further north, at the Firth of Forth in modern Scotland. But his Antonine Wall was soon abandoned in 163 CE due to a Caledonian attack. There were also several Roman forts further north of Hadrian's Wall, including Trimontium (in Newstead, near Melrose), which was occupied by Roman soldiers until at least the 180s CE, and possibly even until 196 CE. Just because Scotland was never conquered by Rome, doesn't mean it isn't full of fascinating Roman archaeology and great places to visit!

HADRIAN'S WALL WAS A DEFENSIVE LINE TO KEEP OUT THE SCARY CALEDONIANS!

It definitely looks that way, doesn't it? Having repeatedly failed to conquer the powerful Caledonians and their allies, the Romans — led by Governor Quintus Pompeius Falco — then suffered a Caledonian counter-attack in 119 CE. Just three years later, Hadrian built his wall — so it seems likely the wall was designed to stop that happening again, right? That's what history books used to say, but many experts now disagree!

The problem is that Hadrian's Wall was much too long and narrow to defend properly. Yes, there were 15,000 soldiers there, but they were divided into little gangs of only 50 soldiers per mile: too few to resist an enemy army. In 181 CE, the Caledonians proved this by attacking the wall and causing lots of damage! Also the tops of the walls weren't flat, so it would have been really hard to stand on them and fight. What's more, Romans preferred fighting in formation, up close and personal with swords and javelins, but you can't do tactical formations while wobbling on a narrow, sloping wall. You'd just fall off!

Archaeologists have found very little evidence of fighting. A defensive barrier would surely have had tonnes of arrowheads, spear tips, shields and swords strewn nearby. But there's not much of this at Hadrian's Wall.

And if the wall was meant to shield Romans from a ferocious enemy, you'd expect the builders to be under constant attack during construction. But we hear of no such problems. You wouldn't build a treehouse if there was a wolf snarling under the tree! So I think it must have been safe enough for the Roman builders to spend 6-10 years out in the open — which makes the defensive line theory very doubtful.

THE PEOPLE NORTH OF THE WALL WERE CALLED PICTS

No, not when the wall was first built! There were nine tribes resisting Roman rule in the area we now call Scotland. In 122 CE, the Romans used the name Caledones for the largest of the tribes. Later records also refer to the Maeatae, possibly two tribes joining forces against Rome. However, it wasn't until the very late 200s and early 300s CE that historical texts mention Picts and Scots. Picti meant "painted people", and the Scotti likely came to Scotland from Northern Ireland.

MYTH BUSTER 6

HADRIAN'S WALL WAS BUILT TO SEPARATE THE ROMAN EMPIRE FROM THE CALEDONIANS

Possibly! The ancient history book *Historia Augusta* says it was built to 'divide the barbarians from the Romans'. However, this very weird book was written 200 years later and might even be a made-up novel! Also, the word 'divide' is intriguing – was the wall a massive territorial marker, saying: 'This is our land; that's yours'? The Romans kept invading the land beyond the wall, so it's not as if they were willing to stick to the agreed boundary!

MYTH BUSTER 7

HADRIAN'S WALL WAS UNIQUE IN THE ROMAN EMPIRE

Not quite. It was the Roman Empire's biggest ever wall, but they also built ones in Germany, Syria, Algeria and Egypt. Hadrian was partially inspired by the Long Walls built by the ancient Greeks.

MYTH BUSTER 8

THERE WERE SPEAKING TUBES ON HADRIAN'S WALL SO SOLDIERS COULD TALK TO PEOPLE FAR AWAY

Definitely not! This myth was made up by a poet in the 1600s. In truth, Roman soldiers sent each other letters by horseback messenger, like those we saw at Vindolanda Fort.

MYTH BUSTER 9

HADRIAN DESIGNED THE WALL HIMSELF

OK, this one might be true! Hadrian helped decide how big the wall would be, along with a team of clever architects and engineers. Some people think the wall got thinner midway through construction because Hadrian visited Britain and realized it didn't need to be so big, after all.

MYTH BUSTER 10

HADRIAN'S WALL WAS PAINTED WHITE

Maybe! There is evidence of a little bit of whitewash (a kind of paint) on a single block at a place called Peel Gap, and there's a tiny bit of plaster at Denton. These are 32 miles apart, on opposite sides of the wall. So there might have been painted decoration all the way along, or only in certain places. We're not sure!

ENOUGH MYTHS... WHAT DO YOU THINK THE WALL COULD HAVE BEEN FOR?

There's lots of theories about what it could have been for, like keeping out robbers or to show off power. There's lots of places for people to cross the wall, so I like the theory that the wall was like airport customs best. The soldiers were there checking that traders had the right paperwork and collecting taxes from everyone, and stopping robbers and bandits from crossing in either direction.

Fascinating stuff, Emma! But, as impressive as Hadrian's Wall is, I think we've spent long enough up here on the northern edge of Roman Britain. Let's head back down south, where things are so peaceful nowadays we can jump forward 50 years, to see what life is like in the bustling new capital ... Londinium!

15
LIVIN' IT LARGE IN LONDINIUM

We've landed in 170 CE, and although the unconquerable Caledonians are still causing headaches up north, elsewhere in Britain things are looking pretty good. Indeed, people are moving here from all over the Roman Empire because there is money to be made. And perhaps the busiest, most bustling place of all is Londinium, Britain's growing capital. Founded in the late 40s CE, and then trashed by Boudica in 61 CE, it's bounced back to become home to 60,000 people, and they are doing their best to enjoy themselves!

So, let's put the *fun*dinium into Londinium and take in the sights, sounds and smells (well, hopefully not too many smells) as we try to fit in with the fashionable crowd.

YOUR GUIDE TO THE LONDINIUM LIFESTYLE

FOR HIM AND FOR HER!

Are you a recent immigrant to Britannia? Or a country bumpkin who is new to town life? Here's a handy guide to living your best life in fashionable Londinium!

WHAT TO WEAR?

If you've moved here from sunny Africa, Syria, Asia or even southern Gaul, you might be in for a bit of shock. You can still look good, but Britannia weather isn't your friend!

ADVICE FOR GENTS

* Ditch the togas! Almost everyone wears a knee-length tunic.
* For extra warmth, add a baggy woollen cloak with chunky square sleeves, and a fancy brooch to complete the look!

- If it's raining (of course it is!), pop on your waterproof leather hoody – choose a long one (the *caracalla*) or a short one that sits on your shoulders (the *birrus Britannicus*). Fabulous!
- If your legs get cold, try woollen leggings or leg wraps to go with your leather sandals.

ADVICE FOR LADIES

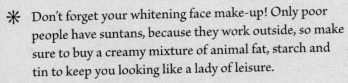

- No underpants, obviously! You're not an uncouth barbarian. But you can wear a tight-fitting bodice under your tunic for extra warmth and modesty.
- Your tunic dress should be very loose-fitting, and come down to your ankles – no longer, or you'll trip on it!
- No hoodies for gals: let people see your elaborate hairstyles!
- Don't forget your whitening face make-up! Only poor people have suntans, because they work outside, so make sure to buy a creamy mixture of animal fat, starch and tin to keep you looking like a lady of leisure.
- Stay warm with a rectangular cloak, and accessorize your tunic with fetching brooches (*fibulae*) pinned on both shoulders. The latest fashionable designs are shaped like hares, cockerels, axes or shoes.

WHERE TO SHOP

* For the best local produce, try the wine merchants. Romans have started growing grapes here in Britannia, and it tastes surprisingly good! Londinium is also full of shops selling foreign goods. You can even get garum sauce imported from Antipolis in south-eastern Gaul!

* For handcrafted goods, visit the different districts for leather workers, potters, blacksmiths, carpenters, butchers, bakers, glass blowers and textile weavers.

* Feeling peckish? Londinium offers plenty of roast beef and fish dishes. Pork is pricier, and you'll only get lamb or goat in the countryside. Wheat and barley cakes make a cheap snack.

MUST-SEE ENTERTAINMENT

* The hottest ticket in town is for the impressive amphitheatre that seats over 6,000, recently upgraded from wood into stone. Don't miss the gladiator fights, thrilling games and violent beast shows. Londinium doesn't get many lions or tigers (the scariest local creatures are badgers!), but ferocious wild bears are imported from Caledonia, and they always put up a fight in the arena.

* Londinium doesn't have a chariot-racing circus or a theatre, but you can visit Camulodunum for those.

STAY HEALTHY!

✳ Of course, Londinium offers a wonderful array of *thermae*. Bathhouses are the perfect places to keep yourself clean, make friends, do business deals, strike up a romance and work up a sweat! Be warned, you bathe naked, and there's no security guard in the locker room, so your clothes might be stolen!

✳ Ladies, if you accidentally rub make-up into your eye, ask for a travelling *oculist*. Britannia is renowned for its eye doctors, who carry marvellous brass boxes filled with ointments, salves and lotions on special sticks to rub onto your infected eyes. These *collyria* sticks are made from fancy ingredients including myrrh, saffron, poppy, aloe plant, vinegar, frankincense, copper, lead and zinc. Only the best in Londinium!

> That's your guide to living it up in Londinium. Enjoy your time in the city, and tell all your friends to come too – there's plenty of room!

EYE DON'T BELIEVE IT!

You wouldn't have found a fashion magazine in Londinium, but everything in it is true! Posh ladies loved to glam up – incredibly, archaeologists found a tin of make-up cream in Southwark, dating to 150 CE, with fingermarks still visible where the last user had scooped some out! There were thermae baths at Huggin Hill, Cannon Street and Shadwell. Speaking of health, for some mysterious reason, Roman Britain had way more eye doctors than other places in the empire. We have found loads of their oculist kits and collyria sticks.

Londinium is the biggest town in Britain, but it's not all fashion and fun. Most people live in small two-room *tabernas*, with gravel floors, not much heating and no indoor toilets! Poor people's houses are made of timber and wattle and daub, beneath a roof of thatch or wooden shingle, and these homes rot away and need rebuilding after ten years.

Wooden strips and soil/dung/straw!

By contrast, richer Londoners treat themselves to fancier pads built from stone, with mosaic floors, copper pipes for running water, indoor latrines and underfloor heating – how swish! In fact, the only thing missing to make this the perfect home is a cuddly pet...

PET PALS

Actually, the Romans did have pets! Archaeologists have found lots of paw prints on floor tiles, from where animals walked on the wet clay before it dried. Dogs were the most popular pets; fashionable Romans preferred yappy little lapdogs rather than a big working dog. The rich also had pet cats, fish, eels and birds. Ravens and crows have been found carefully buried in Roman graves, which suggests they were beloved pets. One raven even had an injured wing that had been healed by a loving owner!

Maybe I should get a dog instead!

Well, that was a lovely trip to Londinium. By the look of all those fashionable clothes, bustling shops and fun entertainments, Roman Britain really seems to be thriving in a time of peace and prosperity. I wonder how long it will last?

16
CHAOTIC COMMODUS

55 BCE   0 CE   100 CE   200 CE   300 CE   409 CE

We've reached 180 CE, and I don't want to jinx it but … things are really calm in Roman Britain, and in the Roman Empire as a whole! Sorry, I know I promised you a chaotic history, but this is the era of the Pax Romana, when the empire is so powerful that everything just runs very smoothly (well, *mostly*!). It's been aaaaaaages since we heard about any rebellions, plagues, invasions or assassinations.

Since 27 BCE
Pax = peace

That's because the current emperor, Marcus Aurelius, is a truly great ruler. In fact, he's the fifth impressive emperor we've had in a row. That must be a record! OK, sure, those defiant Caledonians remain a concern up in the north, and another 5,500

These are the Five Good Emperors: Nerva, Trajan, Hadrian, Antoninus Pius and co-rulers Marcus Aurelius and Lucius Verus. Lucius Verus died young, so only Marcus Aurelius gets remembered!

troops from Sarmatia have just been sent to guard Hadrian's Wall, but it's no big deal. Apart from that, Roman Britain is really thriving.

Sarmatia is a huge chunk of land that now stretches from Ukraine to Hungary.

So, yeah, I guess this chapter will be short and uneventful—

WHOAAAAAA, THE CHAOS METER JUST BLEW UP!!!

What on earth happened to the Pax Romana?! Here we go again, back into the chaos!

GOODBYE GOOD TIMES!

Marcus Aurelius' famous book on Stoic philosophy, called *Meditations*, is still read by many people today!

Ohhhhh nooooooo, Marcus Aurelius is dead! Out goes the wise philosopher emperor, and in comes his layabout son, Commodus. He doesn't want to write books or do dull government paperwork; he wants to drink, feast, party hard, watch chariot races, rename Rome after himself, and even cosplay as a sword-wielding gladiator in the Colosseum,

He wanted to call it Commodiana!

fighting with a sharp sword against harmless animals and disabled ex-soldiers armed with only soft sponges – that's so unfair!

> Emperor, you really should do some work at some point...

Oof, this is not good! At least Commodus is far away in Rome so his foolish antics shouldn't affect things over here in Britain...

GAAAAH, SPOKE TOO SOON!

Commodus is sending a new governor to Britain, called Ulpius Marcellus – and we're in need of a good

leader. The Caledonians just smashed up Hadrian's Wall, killed an important Roman commander, and burned down three forts! Let's hope Marcellus is a good choice to sort things out, and he can undo some of the damage. Oh, nope, everyone hates him for being an arrogant snob!

He worked long hours to make others look lazy and woke up his officers at 2 a.m. if they hadn't replied to his letters!

BARMY ARMY

What else can Commodus get wrong? Well, he's just let a guy named Perennis take over running much of the empire, and Perennis' first decision is to replace posh commanders in the Roman army with lower-ranked ones. Sounds boring, right? WRONG! It's a HUGE insult to Roman soldiers, who take pride in being led by famous officers from posh families. When news reaches Britain, the soldiers are so furious, 1,500 legionaries march all the way from Londinium to Rome to complain!

These angry mutineers invent a fake conspiracy to get rid of Perennis. They tell Emperor Commodus that Perennis is plotting against him, and wants to make his own son the emperor. Commodus says, "OK!", lets the soldiers murder Perennis and his family, and the satisfied troops return to Britain. END OF STORY, RIGHT?

When soldiers turn against their leader that is called a mutiny.

Ha ha ha! As if!

MORE MUTINY MAYHEM!

Commodus is not impressed that Governor Marcellus let the mutineers leave Britain — so he fires Marcellus and appoints Pertinax instead. Wise choice? OF COURSE NOT, THIS IS COMMODUS WE'RE TALKING ABOUT! Pertinax is a disciplinarian who punishes even the tiniest thing, so the army mutinies again, which makes Pertinax punish the rebels so harshly that they mutiny again (and nearly kill him), but Pertinax survives, and punishes them EVEN HARDER, so they send him a delicious ice cream as a thank you… Just kidding, obviously they MUTINY YET ANOTHER TIME!!!

Eventually Pertinax resigns and returns to Rome as a hero, with Commodus' full support. How does Pertinax repay his emperor? By helping to murder him! Yes, the much-hated-and-totally-useless Commodus gets strangled by his fave gladiator in 192 CE, and suddenly Pertinax is the Roman emperor. All hail Pertinax— NOPE, MY MISTAKE! His bodyguards just murdered him too! ← He only lasted 88 days!

Well, all I can say is we've reached 193 CE, and surely things can't get any more chaotic, right?

Oh Greg, you couldn't be more wrong! Prepare for MAXIMUM CHAOS!!!

17

HOW MANY EMPERORS IS TOO MANY EMPERORS?!

Remember when I said we'd reached peak chaos? I'm a total fool! It looks like 193 CE might turn out to be the most chaotic year yet. For starters, I'm not even sure who's in charge! Emperor Pertinax has been killed by the Praetorian Guard – and now, in an extraordinary move that Rome has never seen before, the Praetorians are holding an exciting auction: whoever bids the most cash gets to be emperor!

A rich politician called Didius Julianus wins the auction, plonks his bum down on his new throne,

These elite soldiers were the emperor's bodyguards. They seem to have forgotten about their job description!

and ... gets murdered only 66 days later by the same soldiers who gave him the job in the first place! Oops.

Are you feeling tired yet? I'm exhausted, and we're not even halfway done with 193 CE! I wish we could head back to Britain to chat about shopping or whatever, but these political earthquakes in Rome are much too important. Whoever wins power will shape Britain's future, so we'd better stick it out!

Despite the emperor job sounding increasingly dangerous, there are three brave candidates desperately scrambling to replace *Dead*ius – sorry, I mean *Didius* – and become the THIRD emperor THIS YEAR. The problem is, none of them actually live anywhere near Rome. Hmm, who to choose?

Roll up, roll up! Welcome to

Emperors-R-Us,

your one-stop shop for all your ruling needs!

We've got lots of choices. Howzabout a governor of Britannia? Maybe a Syrian legate? Or even a Pannonian governor?

Have a look around, and see what takes your fancy!

OPTION 1:

DECIMUS CLODIUS ALBINUS
GOVERNOR OF BRITANNIA

A fine choice for emperor, very popular with his soldiers, not at all cruel like Pertinax, or lazy like Commodus. He comes from a very posh North African family, and his large army in Britannia is famous for battling the Caledonians, so they'll be handy in a war against any rivals!

OPTION 2:

LUCIUS SEPTIMIUS SEVERUS
GOVERNOR OF PANNONIA (MODERN CROATIA)

He might not seem like the most powerful politician, but Severus is a fine soldier and shrewd decision-maker. He's also got a good-sized army. He grew up in North Africa and his ancestors were Phoenicians, the old enemies of the Romans, so it will be quite the turnaround if he ends up as emperor!

OPTION 3:

GAIUS PESCENNIUS NIGER
IMPERIAL LEGATE TO SYRIA

Noted for his distinctive looks and very popular in the eastern part of the empire, but also in the city of Rome. Born in Italy, and from a renowned family, he might have a smaller army than the others, but Pescennius is a fine and traditional choice!

FIGHTING IT OUT

Obviously Romans didn't go shopping for emperors — although given the last one paid for his role, it's not such a crazy idea! No, they decided these things with wars. Much more civilized... In fact, ALL of these rivals actually declared themselves the true Roman emperor, but it would have been a bit of a squish to fit them all on one throne, so they had to settle it with a fight!

That's right, this trio of candidates have hurled themselves into a three-way civil war. Sneaky ol' Severus is proving to be the smartest. When Pescennius Niger tries to declare himself emperor, Severus intercepts his messenger before he can spread the news to Rome. Severus tells Albinus that they should gang up together and share the empire as co-rulers ... but Albinus must agree to stay in Britain. Sounds like a good deal, right?

> Historians call this the Year of the Five Emperors, which is one better than the Year of the Four Emperors in 69 CE but not as chaotic as the Year of the SIX Emperors in 238 CE.

But, while Albinus puts his feet up in Britain, Severus goes to war with Pescennius Niger, kills him, marches on Rome, declares himself emperor, and then tells everyone that Albinus is a TRAITOR! See, I told you he was sneaky!

Eventually, in 197 CE, Severus manages to get rid of his final rival as he defeats Albinus, governor of Britain, at the Battle of Lugdunum and becomes the undisputed Roman emperor. That's two governors of Britain in a row (don't forget Pertinax!) who have tried to become emperor and ended up very, very dead!

It must be pretty weird for the soldiers and civilians back in Britain right now, wondering what on earth is going on and who is in charge. Speaking of which, it's time we head back there, because things are about to get interesting…

Watch out for the Caledonians!

18
SEPTIMIUS SEVERUS THE SEVERING SPLITTER-UPPER!

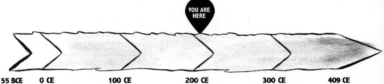

Eleven years have passed, and you'll never guess where the new emperor, Septimius Severus, is heading next!

Oh, you *did* guess? You're obviously getting the hang of this book! Yes, in 208 CE, Severus – the super-sneaky super-soldier – shows up in Britain. He's worried that the next local governor might challenge his power, just like Albinus did. His solution? It's pretty drastic:
Severus severs Britain in half!

OK, not literally – his sword's not sharp enough! But he splits Britain into two different provinces, each with their own governor. The south and west chunk is renamed Britannia Superior, with Londinium as its capital, and the north is dubbed Britannia Inferior, with Eboracum as the capital. The northern province only gets one Roman legion of 5,000 men to defend it, whereas Britannia Superior gets two. And why does Severus do this? Because this makes Britain into two weaker provinces that can't rise up so easily against him. He's obviously learned his lesson from watching Pertinax and Albinus muster huge armies.

→ York.

Hmm, so with its power halved, Britain is once again set to become a quiet backwater of the Roman Empire, right?

BRITANNIA HITS THE BIG TIME

Not at all! Britain was seen as increasingly important. Severus' visit was only the third time an emperor had bothered going to Britain (after Claudius in 43 CE and Hadrian in 122 CE), so it was a huge deal. Lots of the finest foods were imported from Europe and North Africa for Severus and his family to enjoy, and many fancy new buildings were built. A luxury bathhouse was built for the imperial family's travelling court when it stopped at Luguvalium (Carlisle) at the end of Hadrian's Wall. It was discovered in 2017, and in 2023 archaeologists revealed 1,000 exciting finds, including tiles stamped with the imperial insignia, stone inscriptions naming Severus' wife Julia Domna, sculptures, signet rings and a rare lump of purple dye for making his royal toga. Amazingly, this tells us Carlisle was briefly the centre of the entire Roman Empire while Severus stayed there!

So, obvious question: why is Severus trudging all the way up to northern Britain, when he's got a lovely palace to enjoy in Rome, and he's already weakened potential rivals by chopping the province in half? Well, he wants his two sons, Caracalla and Geta, to learn how to be strong warriors, and he reckons the fierce Caledonians are the ideal test of their courage! Recently the governors of Britain have been bribing the Caledonians to behave themselves, but Severus would rather crush an enemy than pay them to go away! Will Severus succeed where no other Roman could? He's going to give it a jolly good try!

CALEDONIAN CONQUEST ... HERE WE GO AGAIN!

Severus marches into Caledonian territory with a huge army of over 40,000 men, intending to conquer the entire island of Britain once and for all. However, like everyone else who's tried this, he soon comes up against the marshes, the chilly weather and the brilliantly cunning Caledonians and Maeatae. They vanish into the countryside, launch surprise ambushes, lure the Romans into traps by tempting them with herds of tasty cows, and refuse to meet in face-to-face battle. Uh-oh, seems like Severus is discovering this isn't as easy as it looks!

The Maeatae were several smaller Scottish tribes joined together who resisted the Roman invasions.

Ooh, a free cow! How udderly delightful!

After two difficult years, Severus gets all the way to the far north of the island – success! Surely he's finally terrified the Caledonians and Maeatae into submission? Satisfied this is mission accomplished, Severus heads back to nice safe Eboracum in 211 CE... And as soon as he turns his back, here come the rebellious Caledonians and Maeatae again – you just can't keep them down! Emperor Severus has been in northern Britain for three years, spending a fortune, and at the cost of many thousands of lives, and yet he's apparently achieved nothing. So, what does the mighty emperor do now? Er ... he dies! Cause of death? A chronic case of → Caledonianitis!

Not a real disease, Greg! It was probably more like exhaustion.

Yes, after reaching Eboracum, Severus becomes the first Roman emperor to die on this island. I guess Severus had always wanted to make history, but probably not like that...

BROTHERLY BETRAYAL

With Severus dead, his two sons, Caracalla and Geta, take over co-running the empire. Perhaps unsurprisingly, they immediately give up in the war against the Caledonians and Maeatae, and rush home to sunny Rome. But once they get there, nasty Caracalla orders his Praetorian

Caracalla was his nickname, taken from the type of hooded cloak that he wore.

He was a very cruel ruler, but the Yorkshire Museum has a nice pot decorated in the shape of his head. These face pots were unique to Roman Britain.

bodyguards to kill Geta, making that the third emperor they've murdered in this book ... they are *literally* the worst bodyguards ever!

With all these brutal civil wars and brotherly betrayals going on in the world of Roman politics, you might expect total panic in Britain. Surely rich people are all burying their treasures in the back garden, stocking up on emergency supplies, and building defensive forts in case they're next in line for a horrible death?

Weirdly, no... They're certainly spending a fortune building stuff, but instead of defences, they're investing in fancy villas. Let's take a look!

19

ALL VILLA, NO FILLER!

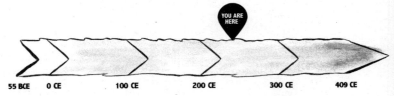

We've reached 230 CE, and while the Roman Empire is sliding into messy chaos, life in Britain's two provinces is actually pretty cushy ... for the rich, at least. The hot new trend is to build lavish villas, but not just as grand palaces for their own enjoyment. No, villas are the central hub for big regional farms, helping to produce food for the ever-growing population.

Maybe we need to treat ourselves to a shiny new villa? Let's take a leaf through the catalogue!

Villas started as luxury palaces, but gradually became more like massive family businesses.

VILLAS IV U

Tired of city living? Long for that fresh country air?
Don't mind stepping in the occasional cow poo?
Then why not swap your town house
for a luxurious country villa!

Here at Villas IV U, we guide you through
everything you need to know about building your
own villa. Just follow these handy steps!

STEP 1:
CHOOSE YOUR BUDGET

Villas are no longer reserved for super-rich Romans! If you've made good money in business, or you've inherited some cash, you too can get on the villa housing ladder – they're not all massively expensive. And by growing food, they actually bring in money, so they basically pay for themselves!*

*They absolutely do not pay for themselves; you still need lots of money to build one.

STEP 2:
PICK A LOCATION

Worried about missing gladiator fights and the latest plays? Country living doesn't mean missing out on town life! Just pick a nice bit of fertile farmland a couple of hours away by donkey cart, and you'll be in the centre of the action in no time!*

*Villa must be near a main road, or travel will be very tricky. Donkey not included.

STEP 3:
SET A SIZE

Get an architect to help you pick out a size and style of villa. In modern Britannia, we're all about that sleek, simple rectangle, maybe with a couple of wings on the front. Size is up to you* – you can keep it modest (4–6 rooms), go medium (8–14 rooms, with upstairs bedroom), or SUPERSIZE IT (like Villa Regis Cogidubni, with its 100 rooms!).

*And the size of your wallet!

DON'T FORGET THE ESSENTIALS:

A hypocaust to heat the kitchens, bedrooms and bathhouse.

A massive granary to store all the grain your farm produces.

A bathhouse – this is where you and your farm workers will socialize. Your villa is like a tiny country in the countryside – you could be like a miniature emperor!*

* Villas IV U takes no responsibility for customers being murdered like a hated Roman emperor.

STEP 4:
INTERIOR DESIGN

Once it's all built, don't forget to decorate – nobody wants a vanilla villa! It's trendy to have your walls plastered in red, green and yellow tones – a classic, classy decor. And remember there's no better way to make your villa pop than with gorgeous mosaics.

SO DON'T DELAY, START BUILDING YOUR VILLA TODAY!

BUILDING SUCCESS

That catalogue might be made up, but it's true that over 400 Roman villas have been found so far in England and Wales (including 15 on the Isle of Wight!). Their number increased rapidly in the 200s CE, even though this was a time of political chaos in the rest of the empire. Villas were the centre of a community. If there was a bad harvest, workers might rely on the villa's grain stores to help them survive — quite a responsibility! Villa Regis Cogidubni — or Fishbourne Palace, as we call it today — is the biggest villa ever found in Britain. You can visit the ruins!

MAGNIFICENT MOSAICS

If you do fancy getting yourself a villa, snazzy mosaics are a must! These are decorative artworks made from thousands of tiny tiles, and the Romans are renowned for them. Mosaics used to be simple patterns in black and white, but in the 200s CE everyone wants bigger, better, brighter and bolder. Scenes from ancient Greek legends are very popular in mosaics — it's super fashionable to depict squabbling gods, vivid sea monsters, an iconic battle scene from the *Iliad*, and anything else that just shouts: *"I've been to Athens, darlings, and I feel fabulous!"*

An epic ancient Greek poem by Homer.

Mosaics are hugely complicated to make, which is why they're a real status symbol for the wealthy. A master designer draws the scene on paper, then craftsmen turn this plan into reality. It's a very technical job that requires attention to detail, otherwise you might accidentally get a gladiator with fins for arms and a dolphin with a sword for a head!

Some artists signed their work – not with a written signature, like a painter, but with certain patterns.

How many times, Marcus?! Gladiators don't have flippers!

Talking of good ideas going horribly wrong, we'd better head back to Rome. I think it's all kicking off again!

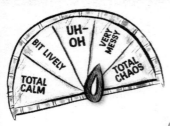

20
WHO'S THE BOSS?!

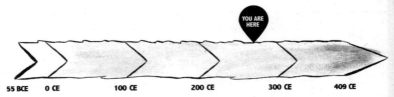

Stop everything: I have HUGE news! While we were building our villa, the Roman Empire descended into chaos … again! It's now 260 CE, and since we were last in Rome, an unbelievable NINETEEN emperors in a row have met a grisly end! I mean, that's just bonkers?!

Where did we leave things? Ah, right, Emperor Caracalla was in charge, wasn't he? He was the one who came to Britain with his dad, Severus, and then murdered his brother, Geta. Yeah, well, the key news is that Caracalla also got murdered, while <u>going to the toilet</u> (awkward!). Ever since then, it's been tremendously popular to kill Roman emperors – just look at this list of lots of (but not all!) the recent deaths!

A disloyal soldier killed him while his guard (and his underpants) was down!

REIGN	EMPEROR	CAUSE OF DEATH
211–217	Caracalla	MURDERED BY OWN SOLDIERS
217–218	Macrinus	KILLED BY A RIVAL (ELAGABALUS)
218–222	Elagabalus	MURDERED BY OWN BODYGUARDS
222–235	Severus Alexander	MURDERED BY OWN SOLDIERS
235–238	Maximinus Thrax	MURDERED BY OWN SOLDIERS
238	Gordian I (father) & Gordian II (son)	DIED BY SUICIDE KILLED IN BATTLE
238	Pupienus & Balbinus	MURDERED BY OWN BODYGUARDS
238–244	Gordian III	KILLED IN BATTLE
244–249	Philip the Arab (father) & Philip II (son)	KILLED IN BATTLE BY A RIVAL MURDERED BY OWN BODYGUARDS
249–251	Decius (father) & Herennius Etruscus (son)	KILLED IN BATTLE
251	Gallus & Hostilian (son of Decius)	HOSTILIAN POSSIBLY MURDERED
251–253	Gallus (same guy as before!) & Volusianus (son)	KILLED BY OWN SOLDIERS
253	Aemilianus	KILLED BY OWN SOLDIERS
253–260	Valerian	CAPTURED BY PERSIANS AND EXECUTED

Nineteen dead emperors is a worrying sign of huge problems in the Roman Empire, with the top job now being more dangerous than tightrope-walking across a volcano while juggling chainsaws! And that's not all. There are plagues; rival Roman legions keep declaring their own generals as emperor; AND the empire is being attacked on three sides, by three enemies! These "barbarian" attacks, especially in the east by the powerful Persians, could have huge consequences for Britain. After all, if all the money is being spent defending the east of the empire, does that leave Britain's two provinces vulnerable to attack in the west?

> The Romans called basically everyone barbarians, except Egyptians and Greeks. It was originally a Greek insult against foreigners whose languages sounded to Greeks like nonsense "bar-bar" noises. Funnily enough, the Greeks called Romans barbarians!

But now, at last, I think we've got a leader who can fix this crisis: Emperor Gallienus. He took power when his dad, Emperor Valerian, was captured and killed by the Persians. (Some claim they forced him to drink molten gold – OUCH!) Gallienus has managed to crush a couple of rebellions, reform the Roman army, and – most importantly – keep breathing! Perhaps Gallienus will be the sensible, successful leader Rome has needed for ages?

> Historians call this time period the Crisis of the Third Century. The empire was getting too big and money was losing its value!

LIVE 260 CE

ROMAN EMPIRE NEWS NETWORK

BREAKING NEWS

We interrupt this book to bring you breaking news that a general called Postumus has killed Emperor Gallienus' son! We are hearing that Postumus' soldiers have declared Postumus emperor of Rome and all its provinces!

WAIT ... NO! Roman Empire News can now confirm that Postumus doesn't want the whole empire; he's only claiming Gaul, Germania, Iberia and both Britannias. In fact, he's rebranding them all as a new Gallic Empire, separate to the Roman Empire!

So, now there's ... uh ... two different empires? Er ... do we have to rebrand too? Welcome to Gallic Empire News, I guess?

WELCOME TO THE GALLIC EMPIRE

New emperor declared by his soldiers, claims land ...

WELCOME TO ~~ROMAN~~ GALLIC BRITAIN!

Whoaaaa! It looks like all this chaos in the Roman Empire really has impacted Britain in a big way – the two provinces have suddenly been pulled into the weird new Gallic Empire under Emperor Postumus, much to Emperor Gallienus' annoyance! How will people here react to this sudden switch-over? Oh ... people are surprisingly fine with it! They're putting Postumus' face on coins and seem pretty unbothered about not being Romans any more. Maybe they're tired of all the chaos?

Postumus basically snatched a new empire made up of land in modern-day France, Germany, the Netherlands, Spain, Portugal and Britain.

WHAT CRISIS?

Just a quick warning, Greg! This Crisis of the Third Century WAS real, but lots of our sources were written 100 to 250 years afterwards by people who weren't there at the time! The earliest writer was Aurelius Victor, the last was Zosimus, and in between them was an unknown writer churning out a bunch of weird, made-up stories in a book called the *Historia Augusta*. This time was very messy, but maybe we shouldn't trust everything you just wrote!

Thanks for the warning, Emma, but I'm more worried about needing to rename this book *Gallic Britain Gets Rowdy!*

Actually… NOPE! Never mind, it seems Emperor Gallienus has just been murdered by a rival, followed almost immediately by Postumus (killed by his own soldiers – this is becoming a common theme!). It was fun while it lasted – but here comes the Roman Empire to reclaim its territory. Bye-bye, Gallic Empire! Hello again, Roman Britain!

Emperor Aurelian defeated the Gallic Empire and made Britain Roman again in 274 CE.

21

EMPERORS EVERYWHERE, ALL AT ONCE!

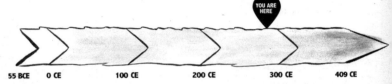

Right, so is everything back to normal now? Not quite! Britain might be back in the Roman Empire, but we're in 284 CE and the new emperor, a chap called Diocletian, is making some big changes. He's exhausted with all the rebellions and attacks on the empire's borders, so he's doing something drastic. Remember when Severus snipped Britain in half? Well, Diocletian is doing that to the ENTIRE Roman Empire!

Yep, the empire is way too big to manage, so he's putting the western half (including Britain) under the control of a soldier named Maximian, and Diocletian is

146

ruling the east. As they're sharing power, they'll both be called Augustus instead of emperor.

> Augustus was the name of Rome's first ever emperor; this is a tribute to him.

All right, now we've got a nice, manageable eastern and western empire, let's get back to a calm, normal book about Roman Britain— OH, NOW WHAT?!

LIVE 286 CE

More BREAKING NEWS

Incredible reports are coming in that Britannia has rejected western Rome and instead broken away to become its own independent British Empire! The new Augustus, Maximian, put a man called Carausius in charge of defending the seas around Britannia from pirates – but it seems Carausius has become a pirate himself, and stolen the entire island! All hail Carausius, the new, uh ... British emperor, I guess?

British Empire News

LONG LIVE THE BRITISH EMPIRE!

Carausius steals island

SERIOUSLY?! This book is exhausting... OK, so we had a Roman Empire, then a Gallic Empire, then a Roman Empire again, then a Western Roman Empire, and now we've got a British Empire? Fine, whatever, so long as it doesn't keep changing—

LIVE 296 CE — Even More BREAKING NEWS

WESTERN ROMAN EMPIRE NEWS

CHAOS IN THE BRITISH EMPIRE!

After seven years of rule, Emperor Carausius has been stabbed to death by his adviser, Allectus, who has now become the new British emperor, and— WAIT, THE ROMANS ARE ATTACKING ALLECTUS! Sources are confirming that Allectus is also dead, and the Romans have restored Britannia back to the Western Roman Empire! And now they are splitting it into FOUR different provinces!

LONG LIVE THE WESTERN ROMAN EMPIRE – AGAIN!

Allectus dead, Rome back in charge

What's that?! There's even bigger news coming from Rome? I can't handle this. I quit!

HOW TO SPLIT UP AN *ALREADY* SPLIT-UP EMPIRE!

How are you feeling? Need a nap? Me too! There's a lot to keep up with, and we're not done yet: Britain is now split into FOUR provinces, to stop any leader getting too powerful and launching another rival empire! And talking of splitting things up, let's return to Emperor Diocletian, who only recently halved the empire because it was too big. Well, he's decided it's *still* too big and hard to manage! So he's bringing in even more rulers in a new system called the *Tetrarchy*, which is where you play Tetris with falling blocks from Hadrian's Wall, and...

They were called Britannia Prima, Britannia Secunda, Flavia Caesariensis and Maxima Caesariensis.

BEEEEEEEP! BEEEEEEP!

ACCURACY ALARM

FOUR'S A CROWD

No, Greg! Tetrarchy is a Greek word meaning "power shared between four people". It was a way of sharing responsibility across the huge empire. Diocletian and Maximian were the two senior Augustus rulers, but there were now also two junior Caesars as well. Diocletian was based in Turkey, and he was the most important of all. The other rulers were based in Milan (north Italy), Serbia and Germany. So, weirdly, nobody was ruling from Rome any more, even though it was the Roman Empire!

I'll be honest, if this Tetrarchy thing doesn't work, I'm worried the Roman Empire might collapse entirely, due to its huge money problems. But actually, it looks like Diocletian's bold idea is paying off! Amazingly, the Tetrarchy is slowly rebuilding the economy and helping to stop rebellions in Rome's far-flung provinces. Things are calming down so much, in fact, it might be possible for one emperor to rule the whole empire by himself again.

But who would be brave enough to take on that incredibly difficult challenge? Oh, hang on, here he comes now!

FACT FILE: CONSTANTINE

Constantine is the son of Constantius – who defeated Allectus and brought Britain back into the Western Roman Empire. Constantine grew up in the eastern empire, but followed his father to Britain, and when his dad died here in 306 CE, the loyal Roman soldiers in Eboracum (York) immediately declared Constantine their new emperor. Good news for him, bad news for the other Romans claiming power for themselves!

Yes, Constantine is a bold and impressive Roman keen to rule. But it's not that simple – there are a few others who feel the same! I fear we've not got space in the book for all the battles. Hmm, what to do? I know, let's use the fast-forward button! Hold on tight...

FAST-FORWARD BUTTON

Constantine claims he's the new western Augustus, but a guy named Severus is actually next in the queue. Uh-oh, we know where this is going...! Over in the eastern half of the empire, the new senior emperor, Galerius, finds out about the rivalry and is furious, but, to calm stuff down, he says Constantine can be the western Caesar (junior emperor) and Severus can be the senior western Augustus. So many confusing job titles! Buuuuuuttttt then Maxentius, son of Maximian, says, "No way! I should be the emperor!" So he gangs up with his dad, captures Rome, kills Severus and fights Galerius. Now Maximian turns on Maxentius (his own son!), but can't defeat him, so runs away to ask Constantine for help. But then Galerius and Maximian both die, so Constantine has a massive war with Maxentius and kills him at the very famous Battle of Milvian Bridge. This means Constantine becomes the emperor of Western Rome. The end! OW, MY BRAIN HURTS!!!

Oof, that was a wild ride! However, at least it's made things simple again. All those battles and beaten rivals mean the Tetrarchy is dunzo! No longer is Rome ruled by four emperors; we're back to having just Augusti. Much simpler!

Constantine is now the emperor of the Western Roman Empire, and he's quietly hoping to one day grab the eastern part too. But first he's bringing another massive change, because unlike recent Roman emperors who have cruelly (persecuted) Christians, Constantine is ditching the Roman gods, and converting to Christianity! What huge news. Let's find out more!

This means they were harassed and punished for their beliefs.

22
CONSTANTINE'S CHRISTIANITY CONVERSION

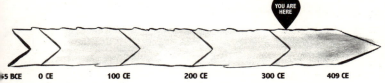

After all that fast-forwarding, we've reached 313 CE, and Emperor Constantine seems to be doing a (pretty great) job ruling the Western Roman Empire, including the four provinces of Britain. During one of his recent battles, Constantine apparently saw a shining cross in the sky, which he believed was the Christian God guiding him to victory. Ever since, Constantine has been inspired to spread Christianity everywhere.

↑ He's actually known these days as Constantine the Great, so yeah, he is!

And that includes here in Britain! In fact, a few Christians have been quietly living in Britain for a while, because it's been a bit safer for them to worship and preach here than in other parts of the Roman Empire, but now Constantine wants to make Christianity a properly legal religion.

> True, but there were still three British Christians executed in this time: St Alban, St Julius and St Aaron.

Constantine is much too busy to pop back to Britain to say hello. (He's in Italy, secretly planning to capture the eastern empire and rule over the whole thing on his own – shh!) But if he'd taken the time to send us a postcard, it might have said something like this!

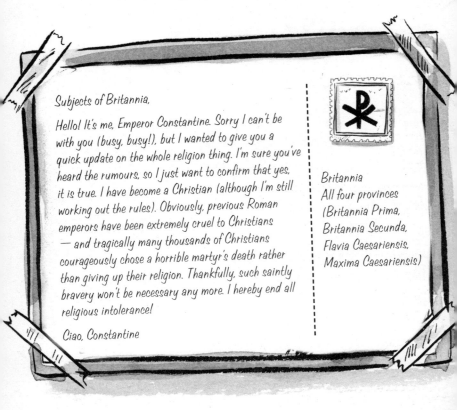

Subjects of Britannia,

Hello! It's me, Emperor Constantine. Sorry I can't be with you (busy, busy!), but I wanted to give you a quick update on the whole religion thing. I'm sure you've heard the rumours, so I just want to confirm that yes, it is true. I have become a Christian (although I'm still working out the rules). Obviously, previous Roman emperors have been extremely cruel to Christians — and tragically many thousands of Christians courageously chose a horrible martyr's death rather than giving up their religion. Thankfully, such saintly bravery won't be necessary any more. I hereby end all religious intolerance!

Ciao, Constantine

Britannia
All four provinces
(Britannia Prima,
Britannia Secunda,
Flavia Caesariensis,
Maxima Caesariensis)

Hello, Britannia, me again!

I hear you want more details about the Christianity thing, and what it means for you. OK: the eastern emperor, Licinius, and I have made Christianity fully legal in both halves of the Roman Empire. So, you can keep on building new churches, electing new bishops, training new priests, and preaching from the Bible. But the great thing is I won't punish those of you who still worship the old Roman gods. I'm a nice, tolerant guy! Everyone can be a good loyal Roman now. Loyal to me.

All the best,
Emperor Constantine

P.S. Has it stopped raining yet? I don't miss the Britannia weather!

Britannia
All four provinces
(Britannia Prima,
Britannia Secunda,
Flavia Caesariensis,
Maxima Caesariensis)

NOT SO HOLY?

Was Constantine really a Christian? Lots of historians and religious thinkers have wondered this. He did make Christianity legal in the Roman Empire with a law called the Edict of Milan, and he later went to war with Licinius, the eastern emperor, claiming that Christians were being persecuted in the east. But we know he kept worshipping Sol Invictus (the Unconquered Sun) for many years, so he didn't immediately give up on Roman gods! But he was baptized before he died. So it was maybe a political choice to pretend to embrace Christianity early on, but he did truly convert by the end.

Constantine defeated Licinius in 324 CE and showed him mercy, but later had him executed when Licinius tried to get back into power.

It's not just religion that Constantine has been busy with. He's now conquered the eastern empire as well, meaning once again the Roman Empire is ruled by just one emperor. It feels like the glory days again!

And this is all good for Roman Britain. Its four provinces are rolling in more money than Scrooge McDuck and King Midas put together! The farms planted 200 years ago now produce so much food, loads can be exported to other parts of the empire for cash. And that means wealthy farmers are splurging fortunes on villas with snazzy mosaics, or keeping treasure troves of gold and silver coins in their houses. Surely this can only be good news, right?!

23

THE GREAT CONSPIRACY

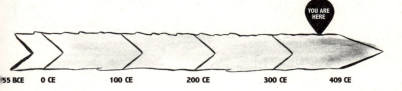

| 55 BCE | 0 CE | 100 CE | 200 CE | 300 CE | 409 CE |

TOTAL DISASTER! Constantine just died, and the empire is split again between his three sons, two of whom go to war with each other – typical brothers! Other wannabe emperors show up with armies and it's basically chaos as everyone scraps for power.

But let's get back to Britain. You know what I said about it being good that Britain is so rich? Maaaaybe I was a teensy bit wrong. Britain's wealth is attracting attention from envious enemies who want to grab the gold, silver, tin, cattle, fancy fabrics, posh villas, yummy foods and nice wines on offer over here. And they plan to get it the quickest way possible – by marching in and stealing it! Luckily, guarding Britain's borders are the crack soldiers of the Roman Empire.

They're the best of the best!

The imperial elite!

The legions of legend!

The...

Oh, maybe not.

Yeah, it turns out Britain's soldiers have become bored, neglected and reduced in number, and are longing for the glory years of trying to murder Pertinax (ah, those were the good old days!). These legionaries used to be terrifying warriors and famously obedient, but now they can be bribed to turn a blind eye, or even switch sides. Which means, here in the year 367 CE, Britain's defences are paper thin, and trouble is coming FROM EVERY DIRECTION!

ENEMIES ON ALL SIDES!

So, how will the new western emperor, (Valentinian,) handle this threat? Well, he's very busy, so he tells an experienced commander named Count Theodosius to sort it out. Off Theodosius goes to Britain, to defend it against foreign attacks. But his men keep deserting him, traitors are giving the enemy key military information, and he soon learns that he is facing FIVE different attackers on THREE different sides – YIKES, that's scary!

Yep, the Romans are facing a Great Conspiracy, meaning different foreign groups – who normally don't talk to each other – are sneakily working together to take Roman Britain down!

> Another emperor who was so impressive, historians call him "the Great".

BEEEEEEEP! BEEEEEEP!

ACCURACY ALARM

NOT-SO-GREAT CONSPIRACY

Don't be so sure! The Romans thought these "barbarians" were working together, but we don't know if there was any clever organization between the various attackers, or if it was just coincidence they attacked a weak target at the same time.

Who are these scary attackers? Let's start in the north, where Hadrian's Wall has never been fully safe even at the best of times! In the north-east, the Romans have started calling their old Caledonian enemies by a new name, the Picts. These Picts are teaming up with the Scotti, who are attacking from the north-west. Meanwhile, in the west, there is a new threat: the Attacotti, who are not to be trifled with! And over in eastern Britain, you've got Frankish and Saxon raiders trashing buildings and mercilessly killing people.

Originally from northern Ireland, the Scotti were based in the western Scottish Highlands.

Basically, Theodosius is surrounded. He must feel like he's in a zombie movie, with bloodthirsty killers trying to get in through every door and window!

The Attacotti were possibly originally from Ireland, the Franks from the Netherlands, and the Saxons from northern Germany and Denmark.

WHAT TO DO?!

How can Theodosius solve this mega-crisis? Well, he cleverly notices the enemy have split up into smaller bands of raiders – so he's not facing big armies, just lots of small gangs! He starts battling his way along the eastern coast of Britain, restoring stolen goods to victims and repairing the damage. Soon Roman soldiers who had run away to become raiders start to sheepishly return. This enlarges Theodosius' army, and – as a lovely bonus – brings fresh information on the enemy's location!

Would you rather fight one giant duck, or 100 normal-sized ducks? Theodosius would deffo choose the second one!

Within a year, Theodosius' army crosses Hadrian's Wall and forces the Picts and Scotti to surrender. But then... DUN DUN DUUUN! He is betrayed by a Roman nobleman named Valentinus, who tries to launch a rebellion against Theodosius! Will all his good work be undone by this sneaky traitor?

Will Britain fall to foreign attacks because the Romans have turned on themselves? NO! Theodosius manages to snuff out the threat in the nick of time... AND RELAX.

HAPPY EVER AFTER

With victory achieved, Theodosius repairs the army forts, enlarges the armies in Britain, and builds new coastal defences to keep out enemy navies and pirates. Amazingly, he's fixed a massive crisis in less than two years! To celebrate, Theodosius looks at Britain's four provinces and decides it needs one more, so he sets up a FIFTH province called Valentia (as a lovely gift to Emperor Valentinian).

By this time, they weren't called provinces – they were dioceses, which is how the Christian Church still divides up regions.

After all that, you'd think a grateful emperor would reward the heroic Theodosius with a lovely holiday, right? Nah – Theodosius gets sent to crush some rampaging tribes in Germania! That's the problem with being good at your job: people keep asking you to do stuff...

So, Theodosius' impressive victory has solved all of Britain's problems for ever, and everyone lives happily ever after in the Roman Empire – hooray!

Oh, hang on, we've still got two chapters left. I guess that means the story doesn't end there? Hmm, maybe postpone the party; let's see what happens next...

24
IT'S ALL GOING A BIT WRONG!

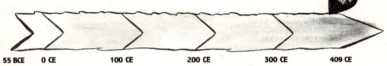

55 BCE 0 CE 100 CE 200 CE 300 CE 409 CE

Oh dear, I was right to cancel that party! There's yet another wrestling match breaking out over who should be Roman emperor, and one of the men leaping into the ring is Britain's top military commander, Magnus Maximus. What is it about bossing it over Britain that makes so many generals think they should rule everything?!

Which means 'the Great, the Greatest' in Latin – what a brilliantly boastful name!

Anyway, Maximus scoops up loads of troops and takes them to Gaul to fight one of his rivals, leaving only a few thousand legionaries rattling around the five provinces of Britain, like pennies in a tin pot. No worries, it's not as if Britain has been under constant attack from foreign raiders for the past few decades, eh? Oh, hang on… YES, IT HAS! Maximus borrowing Britain's army for his foreign trip is like leaving a key in the lock and a sign on the front door saying: "Hello, thief! I am away for a while; all the good stuff is in my bedroom, and there are snacks in the fridge!" You're gonna get robbed, aren't you?

And it's not just an undefended Britain that's now at risk. The entire Roman Empire is under attack from so many directions, and from so many peoples, including the Suebi, Vandals, Alans, Goths, Visigoths and Huns. When Maximus is killed by his rival, Emperor Theodosius, in 388 CE, nobody bothers to replace the troops he took from Britain. Why? Because every soldier is desperately needed elsewhere!

Son of our pal Count Theodosius, who beat the Great Conspiracy – yet another emperor known as 'the Great'!

TRICKY TIMES

How bad have things got for the Roman Empire? Er, pretty bad! The capital city has been forced to relocate to Ravenna, and now communication links to Londinium have been cut off by the Suebi, Vandals and Alans rampaging through Transalpine Gaul. This is terrifying for the Roman officials trying to run Britain's five provinces. Suddenly they aren't getting any messages back from their bosses. They must start to panic. I wonder what kind of letters they're writing?

North Italy – the city of Rome hadn't been the capital since 286 CE!

The region linking southern France and northern Italy.

Dear Emperor,

It has been many months, and we haven't heard from you. I'm just checking in: is there even an empire left? I'm assuming we are <u>still</u> Romans, right? And <u>you</u> are still alive? It would be very nice to hear from you, as we really need your help. We have quite a few problems over here, including:

* We don't have enough soldiers to defend ourselves!

* The Saxons keep attacking us, and so do the Picts!

* Tax collection has collapsed!

* Population numbers are shrinking!

* Wooden buildings are rotting away; bathhouses and sewers are in disrepair!

* Roads need repairing and walls keep falling down!

* Craftspeople don't produce goods and foreign merchants won't trade with us, because nobody can afford anything!

* Dead people aren't being buried properly!

* Roman forts are being abandoned, and local leaders are returning to old hill forts instead!

* Pirates attack our ships when we try to export our grain!

* Did I mention the Saxons and Picts keep attacking us?

Oh, and another thing!

DOWN BUT NOT OUT!

Hang on, Greg! It's true that archaeology shows lots of evidence for towns going downhill, and the Principia Basilica building in Eboracum, where Constantine the Great was proclaimed emperor, was even being used as a barn for pooing, mooing cows! HOWEVER ... many people in the countryside probably continued living normal lives — and now they didn't have Roman legions marching through their field every 20 years, or tax collectors to pay! Farmland wasn't abandoned but farming *was* less intense. Clearly, less food was needed if it wasn't being sold abroad, and the population was falling.

Fair point, Emma!

But without the taxes and grain exports, a once mighty economy is quickly going down the toilet. Nobody is building any fancy villas, and if people do have any spare money, they mostly seem to be hiding it in the ground, so raiders can't steal it!

BEEEEEEEP! BEEEEEEEP! ⚠️

COIN HOARDS 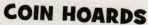 **ACCURACY ALARM**

Actually, we're not sure about that! Archaeologists have found lots of buried *hoards* (collections of silver and gold coins, or other treasure) dating to this time. The Hoxne, Thetford and Mildenhall Hoards are among the most famous. Were these cash stashes hidden from raiders by rich Romans? Were they buried <u>BY</u> successful raiders, who couldn't carry the heavy treasure home, or didn't fancy splitting the loot with their accomplices? Were hoards offered as sacrifices by desperate people hoping to buy divine protection? We don't know! Whoever buried hoards never came back for them, so now they are safely conserved in museums for everyone to marvel at...

Well, whatever coin hoards are for, there's no doubt that things are going wrong in Britain. Who's even in charge here?!

EMERGENCY EMPEROR ELECTION UPDATE!

With no news from Ravenna, the few remaining Roman soldiers in Britain are panicking, so they choose one of their senior officers, Marcus, as an emergency emperor to defend them ... and then they instantly murder him! Luckily, there's another guy called

They didn't like his ideas! ➚

Gratian who ... nope, they've killed him too! (After only four months!) Maybe third time lucky? They now choose Constantine III, simply because he shares a name with the great former emperor. Personally, I'd say better to pick leaders based on their skill and experience, not on what their mum called them, but that's just me...

Is Constantine III any good at the job? Well, uh, sort of. He doesn't die immediately, which is a great start! But then he goes to war with Honorius, the current Roman emperor based in Ravenna, and the two vanish into their epic slog to the death. Meanwhile the people of Britain are wondering where their rulers have gone. This doesn't look good!

25

A BIG, BAD BRITANNIA BREAK-UP

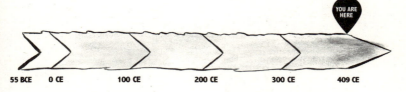

55 BCE   0 CE   100 CE   200 CE   300 CE   409 CE

The year is 409 CE, and everyone is totally ghosting Britain. Imagine being a local leader, wondering if anyone is ever going to send help while attackers circle your shores and your buildings crumble around you. Not fun.

But wait a minute! Emperor Honorius, the rival who has been fighting Constantine III, has finally done the decent thing: he's replied to Britain's panicky messages! And what does he say?

"Look to your own defences."

This is a VERY famous quote, from the ancient writer Zosimus. But some modern historians think he wrote this to Bruttium in Italy, not Britain. Other historians say it WAS Britain. Debate is fun!

This is a polite way of saying: "Sorry, Britain, you're on your own – good luck!"

WHOOOAAAAAA... Did the Roman Empire just dump Britain by text message?! I think it did!

THIS. IS. HUGE.

After 464 years of trying to keep hold of the place, I think Rome just broke up with Britain!

THE END OF ROMAN BRITAIN

Wow, there you have it – Roman Britain is no more! Suddenly, with no armies and no taxes, there is no such thing as a <u>central government</u> to help organize things.

Britain now had a strong Christian community, and it stayed in touch with the Roman Church, at least.

It's now up to local people to gather together and figure out how to make their communities function. Will they try to rebuild the mighty buildings and keep living in the old Roman towns, or abandon them and start again?

> Evidence suggests they abandoned towns, sometimes recycling old stone and materials. They even stopped using coins – and fashion, food and culture all changed dramatically.

Moreover, how will the Britons defend themselves against the oncoming waves of foreign raiders? In fairness, these attacks have started to slow down, perhaps because there's less treasure to steal from a bankrupt Britain! But surely it's only a matter of time before invaders return with large armies to grab what they've wanted for so long?

Meanwhile, the Roman Empire doesn't exactly thrive once it breaks up with Britain. After yet more wars with Goths, Vandals and whoever else shows up to the party, its western empire totally collapses in 476 CE. Only its eastern half – based in Constantinople, the massive capital city founded by Constantine the Great – keeps going for another thousand years, under the new name of the Byzantine Empire.

> Modern Istanbul.

But these stories are for other books! Our ancient history of Roman Britain is DONE AND DUSTED. Oof, I don't know about you, but I need a long lie-down in a dark room!

I hope you've enjoyed this hectic race through a thousand years of ancient British history. I think you can see why I called it a *CHAOTIC* history!

But it wasn't just the past that was messy. Emma's expert interruptions have shown that historical truth is slippery, like a squirming eel! That's the thrilling thing about history: it always takes you somewhere unexpected, because historians and archaeologists are still scrabbling around, trying to make sense of the conflicting sources and annoying holes in our knowledge. There are some things we know, and some things we know we don't know … but what if there's loads of stuff that we don't even know we don't know, you know?!

Wonderfully, that means there is always more to find out, more questions to ask, and more holes to poke in the "facts". Asking difficult questions is good! If you'd love to learn more about Roman Britain, there are loads of fantastic museums and sites you can visit, all over the UK. And there are lots of brilliant books, podcasts, websites, TV shows, YouTube videos and even video games that can help you expand your passion. Maybe one day you'll become an ancient historian or archaeologist yourself, and you can tell me all the facts you think I got wrong. (I look forward to it!)

But until then, it's time for Emma and me to say goodbye. And remember, as we go about our daily lives, let's be thankful for all the good stuff we get to enjoy, because we never know when things are about to get …

MEET THE MAKERS

GREG JENNER is a public historian, author and broadcaster. He is best known for hosting the BBC's educational comedy podcasts *You're Dead to Me* and *Homeschool History*. As Historical Consultant to CBBC's BAFTA and Emmy award-winning TV comedy series "Horrible Histories", Greg was in charge of all the history facts for 1,500 side-splitting sketches and songs, and for the spin-off movie. He has written three books for adults, and released his first children's book, *You Are History*, in 2022. Discover more at **gregjenner.com**

RIKIN PAREKH studied art at Camberwell College of Arts and the University of Westminster. When he's not drawing you'll probably find him at the cinema or at Comic Con. You can see more about Rikin at **rikinparekh.com**

MEET THE ROMAN EXPERT

DR EMMA SOUTHON is a Roman historian and writer. She studied ancient history at the University of Birmingham and is the author of four books on Roman history. You can find her online at **emmasouthon.com**

I didn't get into the Romans until I was a teenager because I thought they were just boring army guys. When I was sixteen I learned about Caligula and realized they were horrible and chaotic and very fun. There are so many good stories from the Roman Empire and a lot of baddies. I really love thinking carefully about what stories survive (and which ones don't) and whether they are really true.

Another TOTALLY CHAOTIC adventure awaits ...

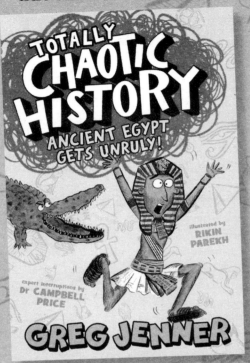

And look out for ...

TOTALLY CHAOTIC HISTORY: THE STONE AGE RUNS WILD!

Available June 2025